Your Key
to the
Akashic Records

Fulfill Your Soul's Highest Potential

JIAYUH CHYAN

Difference Press

McLean, VA, USA

Published 2017

ISBN13: 9781683092070

ISBN10: 1683092074

DISCLAIMER

Cover Design: Jennifer Stimson

Editing: Maggie McReynolds

Author's photo courtesy of Rusty Dyer

For my father,錢星橋, Shing Chiao Chyan.

I wish you could see this book in person,
but I know you are proud of me.

THE UNIVERSAL AKASHIC PRAYER©

Dear Universal Light Beings,

We hold your love, light, and wisdom in our hearts.

Please help us to be a clear channel with complete trust

in our ability to surrender our human judgment.

Please help us to connect with open hearts,

And to know the truth of our existence.

So that we may be of service for the highest good of all.

Author's Note: This is the prayer I received from the Akashic Records for writing this book and it is how I access the Akashic Records. You will learn where it came from and how to use it yourself later on in the book.

TABLE OF CONTENTS

INTRODUCTION

Why Am I Writing This Book?

Do you wish that you had a personal advisor 24/7 to help you with all the questions in your life? Friends are great to talk things over with, but let's face it - you have to figure things out on your own and make your own decisions in the end.

Would you like to hear from your soul about your best next step so you could move forward with confidence in any situation?

You can, if you know how to access your own Akashic Records. When you access your Records, you are able to get suggestions from your soul about the things that you're struggling with and not sure how to handle.

Maybe you've heard about using prayer to access the Akashic Records, but the prayers you've read don't resonate with you. Do you think you are not doing it right?

Have you already connected with your Akashic Records but not sure how to get the most out of this powerful resource?

Would you love to be able to access your own Akashic Records, know that your answers are there, and learn how to use this guidance effectively?

That is why I am writing this book!

I have met so many amazing people on my spiritual journey. Many of them told me over the years that I was going to write about it or asked me, "When are you going to write a book?" I've always just chuckled because it seemed impossible to me to write a book in my non-native language.

In mid-2015, three people asked me about my book within a week. That's when I realized that all the questions weren't just a coincidence. So one day, I decided to stop saying no to the Universe about writing a book. That same day, I received an email from a local magazine about a book collaboration opportunity. Knowing that was the sign from the Universe to tell me to get moving, I signed up to write a chapter for a book called *Essential Healing for Your Spirit and Soul.*

In that chapter, "Putting Myself First," I shared my struggles while on my spiritual journey as a resource to help people navigate their lives. That was the beginning of my journey of writing in English. I was still a pricing actuary with an insurance company then.

Something happened during the writing of that chapter. It was the first time that I consciously took a look at the last decade of my life, the ten years since I started my spiritual journey. I couldn't help but think that if there were someone out there who was going through what I went through, my writing would let them know they weren't alone.

Since then, I have written blog posts for my business, and I've written another chapter, "Finding Inner Peace with Sacred Geometry," for my second book collaboration, *Recipes for Living HCC Editions,* to teach people how to use Sacred Geometry as a meditation tool. The part of me that wants to share what I know with people continues to become stronger and stronger.

When my Akashic Records first urged me to write this book, I resisted. "Who am I to write this book?" I thought.

When the Records provided me with the information of a new prayer, I resisted. The challenges and responsibilities of introducing a new prayer into the world intimidated me.

Finally, my fears were overcome by trusting that the information in my book will be helpful to people who have been searching for it.

The Akashic Records have literally transformed my life. I am living a life that I never thought possible, and I want that for you as well. It is with a servant's heart that I am writing this book. I hope it will help you with your journey.

Who Am I?

I was born and raised in Taiwan and strongly influenced by Chinese culture, values, and beliefs. In 1988, I came to the US to attend graduate school. My subsequent marriage changed me from a confident career woman into a timid prisoner over the course of 17 years.

I finally found the courage to file for the divorce and follow through with it in 2005. I struggled with grieving for the child I lost through a miscarriage, the end of my marriage, and the guilt of not being there for my father's funeral. All of these sorrows just about brought me to my knees, even as I continued to manage everyday tasks.

My spiritual journey began when, prompted by a mix of devastation, skepticism, and curiosity, I started seeking help and answers. Blown away by my first energy therapy experience in March 2006, I went to classes for and started practicing Healing Touch energy therapy on myself. In spite of my analytical mind as an actuary, I soon realized that the energy work helped me manage stress levels and ease difficulties in life in a very profound way. Then the healing began!

Over the next decade, I helped many people with what I had learned from various modalities. Even so, I still went through a period of disbelief and resistance of my gifts. Little by little, I learned to accept me for exactly who I am and embrace gifts from the Universe.

I have been working with the Akashic Records since February 2014 and teaching courses since January 2015. I founded my company, Reaching The Harmony Within to share the tools I have learned with others. Finally, I reached clarity on my true passion. I chose to retire from my two decades in corporate America in July 2015.

In May 2016, I reclaimed my birth name, Jiayuh Chyan, to honor both my heritage and spiritual journey. That's also when I changed my company name to Jiayuh Chyan. Jiayuh Chyan is 錢家鈺 in Chinese. 家鈺 (Jiayuh) is my first name; 家 (Jia) means home or family and 鈺 (Yuh) is a type of precious stone. My name means treasure of the family! My parents named me to express the joy I brought to our family. However, I used the nickname Rosa since I came to the US. I had such a difficult time getting people to say or spell Jiayuh right (it is pronounced Jee-ah-u Chy-an). I was actually embarrassed by my own name!

How Did I Discover the Akashic Records?

One summer about eight years into my spiritual journey, I felt that I needed to find another way to help people in addition to the various energy medicine modalities that I was already offering. I had many clients ask me questions about overcoming obstacles in life, but I had no training to help them. More and more, I wished there was a way I could help them.

I knew I needed a tool that could somehow provide suggestions when my clients were searching for answers, but I also knew that it was not a typical psychic reading. Not sure what I was looking for, I surfed the Internet. I came across Caroline Myss's Sacred Contract Archetype Consultant training program, was excited by it, and bought the Archetype cards. The cards arrived and sat in the drawer for a while. Then I knew it was not for me.

Later that same summer, I came across the Akashic Records while Googling. As soon as I read the description of them from the first website I stumbled upon, I was intrigued.

After reading several online articles, I realized that the Akashic Records were the same as "the Book of Life" that I'd heard about while growing up. I thought the Book of Life was just some made-up stories that older generations told kids about. I could not believe it actually existed. Despite all the articles I read raving about how the Akashic Records have all the information of all the lifetimes and how useful that is for people, I questioned the truth of it. I had never believed reincarnation was real, even though I grew up with this concept in Buddhist culture.

The notion of being able to get help 24/7 seemed to be too good to be true to me. But it would be so empowering if it were! "What if it *is* true?" I thought. "What if it is true that I have had many lifetimes before? What if it is true that people can access the Akashic Records and get information? What if I can get help from my own soul?"

The idea of connecting with my soul was intriguing, but still a mystery to me. Why would I need access to my own soul? Didn't I already have it? I was puzzled. I also doubted that I could do it. "I am just me. Wouldn't a person need some special magical power to do this pretty amazing thing?" I argued with myself.

Anyhow, I Googled some more and found out there were people who could teach me how to do this. Many of them offered online classes. I did not mind online classes, but I was scared by an interview I listened to about taking the next step. The interviewee said that if you let people with bad intentions access your Akashic Records, then they can mess you up. I didn't want to get messed up, so I told myself to forget about it.

Six months later, I went to Massachusetts for a workshop. During a lunch break, I asked the people at my dining table if anyone had heard about the Akashic Records. The owner of the center replied, "Yes, we offer classes at our place. I took the class myself, too. It is pretty awesome. We have a Beginning Class coming up in February next year. Patty is a great teacher."

Needless to say, I could not believe my ears. But I thought I was crazy enough to drive three hours for that workshop as it was. The possibility of me doing that again in the New England winter was close to none. So I abandoned the idea.

The next January, I started giving a family emotional and financial support, which brought incredible chaos into my life every day. Wanting to get away from all the craziness, I decided to attend the upcoming Akashic Records class in Massachusetts just so I could escape the insanity for one weekend. My friend Pat wanted to support me during that difficult time, so she came with me.

It was there, at that first beginners' class, that I met Patty Collinsworth, my very first Akashic Records teacher. I am forever grateful for her love and support throughout my Akashic journey.

Our assigned reading prior to the class was *How to Read the Akashic Records* by Linda Howe, which served as the equivalent of a textbook for us. I read it as asked, and did some practice. The book was fascinating and easy to follow, but like you, I wasn't sure if I did it right because I felt nothing. So I was anxious to find out how the class experience would be different for me than reading the book.

During our drive to Massachusetts for the class, I had shared with Pat my fear of being messed up by someone in the Records. Neither one of us knew what to expect. Therefore, it goes without saying that I was hugely surprised when not only was I able to feel something, I even saw visual images in the "opening of the Records" exercises that Patty led us through in the class.

Trying hard to understand what was happening, I asked Patty a lot of questions, all of which she answered patiently. She also shared with us many of her hands-on experience as examples. Patty looked very young to me; I wondered how she learned to teach this cool thing at such a young age.

Patty helped me understand that the Akashic Records are safeguarded by Light Beings to make sure that the integrity of the Records is never compromised. That was music to my ears! My fears went away.

More unexpectedly, I received advice from my Records that I needed to become a certified teacher like Patty and teach this course. I "heard" this advice as part of a conversation I had with my Records in my mind, during a guided exercise intended to reveal why I had come before the Records at that time. I was so puzzled and confused, thinking, "Where did all of this come from?"

As much as I did not want to believe the advice from the Records to become a teacher, I could not help but wonder: what if it was true? What if I was meant to be a teacher?

I had so many questions! I not only asked Patty questions during the class. I continued to ask after I returned home, via email. I especially wanted to know about Linda Howe's teaching programs, which Patty had gone through. Again, she answered all of my questions patiently and gave me a great deal of support.

Two months later, in April 2014, I decided to sign up for Linda Howe's online teacher training program, and I earned my first teacher certification on October 2, 2014, in a final, in-person training. Through this program, I met

Fran Friedman, Lynne Grobsky, Gwendolyn Hill, and Laura Hosford, who all graduated with me as certified teachers and would become very important to me later on.

I thought I was all set with learning all about Akasha. Little did I know that it was just the beginning of my journey in the Akashic Records. I continued on to join The Akashic Network (TAN), become an Akashic Records certified teacher at TAN, collaborate in curriculum development, and teach TAN's program.

Once again I thought, this has got to be it. This time I should be done with learning all about Akasha. But I was wrong again. Here I am writing this book given by the Akashic Records from yet another level of the Akashic Light!

I now realize that there are infinite dimensions in the Akashic realm. As we grow and nurture our relationship with our Akashic Records, we go deeper and reach new places in the Akasha; the Records always meet us where we are. Therefore, I invite you to keep your perspective open and allow your inner wisdom guide you throughout this journey of your lifetimes. Yes, all of them!

How Have the Akashic Records Changed My Life?

Before I came to the Akashic Records, I already had eight years of experience in working with various energy medicine modalities. I felt my life had already been enlightened and transformed. I was confident that I had already gone through plenty of spiritual growth and awakenings since my divorce. I had no idea that the major shifting was yet to come, with the Akashic Records guiding me through life.

Having 24/7 guidance from the Akashic Records was a life saver for the first three months after I learned how to access them. My life filled with chaos everyday due to the helping hands I extended to that family. There is no doubt in my mind that I would not have made it through that period had I not had the support of my Records.

Looking back on my life since the Records, I chuckle and say there should be a label on the "box": "Warning! Your life will never be the same. Fasten your seatbelt for the transformation of your lifetime!"

In my Energy Medicine work, I had always experienced receiving visual images, but I never thought too much about it. Through my work with the Records, I learned that visual images are the most efficient way for my Records to communicate with me because it is direct, without needing verbal language. So "seeing" is the predominant way for me to receive information. As my skills in the Records improved, I began to receive information by hearing, feeling, and knowing as well.

Since I came to the Records, I have been able to have clarity in even the most difficult situations I've encountered by integrating my ego. It has taken time to integrate my ego with the divine (we will talk about this more later in the book), but I got there (and am still getting there), little by little and layer by layer. I have grown to accept myself so that I can speak up for myself, and because of that, I see the goodness in people without judgment. I listen to my heart more closely. I have found the courage to honor my own spiritual authority even though it means sometimes I have to make painful decisions.

My Records have supported me every step of the way through crisis and milestones ever since. They were instrumental in helping me move on when I needed to: leaving corporate America and, later, moving on from teaching Linda Howe's program.

It was through the Akashic Records that I was reunited with my soul group, the women I mentioned earlier: Fran Friedman, Lynne Grobsky, Gwendolyn Hill, and Laura Hosford. It was the personal and spiritual growth that resulted from my work in the Records that brought me to the realization of the importance of reclaiming my birth name, Jiayuh, and letting go of my nickname, Rosa. And after a devastating house fire, it was the Records that helped me learn how to move beyond my own emotional turmoil and observe my behavior to see the spiritual truth behind the disaster.

The Records have encouraged me to step out of my comfort zone and face the challenges that I'd never thought I could overcome, including writing this book. I am humbled to be of service and to bring this valuable resource into your world.

Why Now?

Choosing to stop teaching Linda's program was one of the toughest decisions that I've had to make. Her work opened the door for me to the Akashic Records, and I would not be where I am without it.

Even though my Records were clear on the subject of leaving Linda's work behind, it took more than courage and trust to follow that particular guidance without knowing how it was going to play out. It was the knowing that I had to do it in order to move forward that helped me make the decision.

I knew in my heart that answering my soul's calling and being one step closer to completing my divine mission of this lifetime was what I wanted to do, even though it meant starting all over, a lot of hard work, and feeling heartbroken over leaving one of my mentors. I officially stopped teaching Linda's program on September 11, 2015, in order to work with a new prayer, the Akashic Access Prayer©. No, it's not the same prayer I opened this book with. More on that in a bit.

The Akashic Access Prayer© (AAP) was received in the Records on July 15, 2015, by my fellow teaching grad Fran Friedman, who founded The Akashic Network (TAN). Fran was then guided to share the prayer with me, Lynne, Gwendolyn, and Laura. Together, the five of us formed the Akashic Network Council of Light (ANCL) and developed a TAN-certified curriculum in group consciousness through collaboration in the Records.

This work as a member of ANCL at TAN was instrumental in taking my understanding of the Records to a deeper level. The classes I taught were so much more robust, with open discussions that met the needs of my students. It also ignited my desire to seek spiritual truth, which I have learned to do more effectively in the Records. This experience definitely led me to the next series of spiritual awakenings.

I have worked with many energy medicine modalities over the years, but since the beginning of 2016, I have been drawn to focus primarily on Arcturian Healing and Sacred Geometry Activation. The Arcturian Healing Method is an upper-dimensional Light and Frequency channeled through the spiritual beings from the Arcturus star system. The Light and Frequency is multidimensional, and can work on many levels of our energy system. Sacred Geometry is repeated geometrical patterns that are the building blocks of our physical world. Each shape is unique in its vibrational resonance encoded with the blueprint of our DNA. Each person has a Sacred Geometry energy field that, when activated, serves as a critical instrument to propel our ascension process. In this book, ascension refers to reaching higher level of consciousness.

All the Arcturian Healing and Sacred Geometry Activation workshops I've facilitated as well as the work I have done on myself have strengthened my connection with the Records. As a result, the Records have helped me to see a much bigger picture than the one that I used to know.

The Records showed me the view from the Universal level, beyond Earth.

In the meantime, the more Akashic Records classes I taught and the more questions I answered for my students, the more I felt the need and desire to share what I knew with more people.

Before I started this book project, I thought I was simply going to write a book about my own journey. You know, just to share my stories with you. In the preparation stage, however, I was made aware that I needed to write a book about the Akashic Records. Then I thought for sure that I was going to write the book using the Akashic Access Prayer©. I even had a good conversation with Fran and got her permission to use AAP in my writing.

Needless to say, it was beyond shocking to me when my Akashic Records informed me that I would be given a new prayer for this book. Immediately, I was overwhelmed with fear. Fear that this was a mistake. Fear of the responsibility that comes with introducing a new prayer to the world. Fear that said, "Who am I to do this?"

The guidance to use a new prayer came through during a routine Akashic Records exchange I had with my friend, Lynne Grobsky. I wanted to refuse this call to service, so I argued with the Records through Lynne and asked why. The answer was: "This is the next step in bringing a new level of Akashic Light into the world." I had so many mixed emotions and could not help crying for a good five minutes.

Poor Lynne was tearing up with me as well.

This book and information that comes with the new prayer, written in the opening pages, is the result of a collaborative effort. It is the sacred contract of a group of people at the soul level to make it happen. All the fellow travelers on the path before me have shown the way so that this new prayer could come through.

I am nothing but a messenger. It is part of my divine mission to share with you what the Records want us to know in this time of human history, so that many who have been searching for this information can have it and continue to move forward for the highest good of all. More than ever before, now is the time for us to reunite with our soul groups, complete life lessons for the ascension process, and help heal the Earth.

Read on, my fellow travelers, and discover for yourself!

CHAPTER ONE

WHAT ARE THE AKASHIC RECORDS?

Reincarnation, Come Again?

Before we can talk about what the Akashic Records are, we need to discuss the concept of reincarnation. We all have a physical body and we all have a soul. Our body is visible, of course, to the naked eye, but our soul is not. While we all know our physical body will die someday, most people don't know for sure what happens to our soul without a body.

I grew up in the Buddhist culture of Taiwan; some people there believe in reincarnation, and some don't. I did not know what to believe, so it had always been a very blurry and gray area to me until my work in the Akashic Records.

Keep in mind, I was an actuary working with numbers and formulas. I did data analysis to solve problems. Everything in my life needed logical, objective proof. From working with my Akashic Records, I know it is true that my soul has reincarnated many lifetimes. It was actually somewhat uncomfortable to realize that in the beginning, and in the back of my mind I thought, "Now what?"

So why do our souls want to reincarnate and live many lifetimes? You see, our soul is invisible as it is pure energy. It is in the body that our soul can experience the things that exist in the physical world. And it is through human emotion that our soul gets to experience feelings. But there is more than that. It is through the school we call "life" that our soul gets to learn from the very ups and downs that will help our soul grow.

Hence before each lifetime, your soul decides what lessons you want to learn this time. It chose you because you are the perfect person to carry out those lessons.

Why We Are All Interconnected at Soul Level

When I first started on my spiritual journey, I didn't understand why people say we are all interconnected as one. In the fall of 2015, I had conversations with different people about our soul, over-soul, and oneness. I spent some time researching these topics, but still couldn't get a good picture, especially the concept of over-soul that encompasses all human souls.

One night, I was flipping through TV channels when this "how the Earth was made"-type show caught my eye. It was on the Science Channel. The show was a combination of fact as well as hypotheses such as the Big Bang Theory. Regardless of whether the Earth was actually made according to that show, it helped me understand the concept of oneness at the soul level.

Imagine the ancient days at the beginning of the Universe, when there was nothing but atmosphere, gas, and energy. In those days, everything was in the form of energy. Then gravity began to bind particles together. However things happened, Big Bang or not, it is scientific fact that atoms bind together to become elements, and elements bind together to become molecules, and then molecules bind together to become matter, which is everything in our physical world.

Therefore it makes total sense that before matter formed to make up our physical world, we all came from the same energy as the Universe. We were one and we are all interconnected at the soul level, even though we are separated today in the physical world as individual bodies.

Scientific fact also tells us that there are other star systems in addition to our own solar system in our Milky Way. Beyond that are other galaxies. So what we can observe from Earth is just a teeny, tiny piece of the Universe.

Now pause for a brief moment and think: what are the odds that our souls have only had lifetimes on Earth?

Yeah – think again!

What Are the Akashic Records?

Akasha is a Sanskrit word. It means sky, space, or open air. It is the basis and essence of all things in the material world. It consists of subtle energies from which all things arise. It is also the constant and enduring memory of the Universe, which holds the record of all that ever happened in life since the inception – on Earth and in the cosmos – and all that is yet to happen.

Some refer to the Akashic field as a field of cosmic information or collective consciousness. The Akashic Records is an energetic or vibrational recording of all thoughts, events, and experiences of our soul through all lifetimes, including past, present, and all future possibilities. Conversely, it also contains our soul's essence and blueprint at inception before being covered up by the experiences and influences of life.

Even though the Akashic Records have been around since the beginning of the Universe, historically access to the Records has been granted only to a very few, highly evolved people. It was because the human race collectively did not have a high enough level of consciousness to use the information wisely for the greater good. Overtime, however, the more mankind has evolved spiritually, the wider the access the Records have granted us.

Every living thing has its own Records. Land, business, buildings, nature, and places all have their own Records. While the Records have currently granted you the right to access your own Akashic Records, it is a privilege and honor to access the Records for others, and therefore much care is needed in doing so. Later in the book, you will learn the guidelines to follow in various situations.

Since it is the Records of all lifetimes, available information is not limited to only lifetimes on Earth. However, as a rule of thumb, any information revealed to us is based on the relevancy to the matters at hand that we are trying to understand, and only when we are ready to know the truth. Anything that is not helpful for our next step would not be shared with us from the Records.

How Do People Access the Akashic Records?

There are many different ways to access the Records. It all depends on what works best for you. Some people get to the Records through meditation. Some use hypnosis. For some people, it happened during an energy healing session. There are also people who can naturally tune in to the Records without any outside means.

There is also the use of a prayer. There are many different prayers available from various organizations and books. It totally depends on which one resonates with you most.

In this book, we are using the Universal Akashic Prayer© with which I opened this book. You'll learn more about it later.

Just Do It! Open Records Exercise #1 – Self

The purpose of this exercise is to dip your toe in the water without being bombarded by information or overwhelmed by expectation. We will go over more detailed instructions later in the book.

- Have the Universal Akashic Prayer© from the beginning of the book on hand.

- Read the prayer once out loud.

- Set the intention that you would like to access your own Akashic Records.

- Visualize the light of your Akashic Records coming down from your eighth chakra (approximately at arm's length when you raise your arms above your head) to your heart. It connects your heart to your will at the solar plexus area (below your heart and above your belly button). It then connects your heart to the divine (above your eighth chakra).

- Use your imagination or your mind's eye (in the middle of your brow) to observe your surroundings. Notice them and let them go.

- Stay in your Records for about three minutes.

- Express gratitude to the Universal Light Beings. Say, "We are complete" out loud to end the exercise.

- Write down whatever your experience was.

Information, Consciousness, and Energy

Information recorded in the Akasha is everywhere. It is inside of us as well as outside of us. You might ask, "So why did I not know about it?" or, "Why have I never felt it?" It is because you never consciously connect with it. The movement of the consciousness to get the information is the energy.

Information in the Akashic Records can be viewed as millions of books on the shelves of a library. If you do not go and get the book, you would not be able to read it, right? And once you get the book, you still have to read it and understand it for the information to be useful. It is just like how you learn in school or anywhere else. Sound simple? It is.

But you wonder: "If everyone has access to their own Records, why do I have to learn how to do it?" The answer is that the information in the Akashic Records resides in a dimension of higher consciousness. If our consciousness level is not as high as the Akasha, then we need a key to help us tune in to the Akashic Realm. The key we use in this book is the Universal Akashic Prayer©.

Intention plays an important role here as it is what makes the consciousness move, sort of like a spark to start the engine of a car. Setting the intention is establishing the heart-mind connection. It gives the mind the ability to tap into and integrate the wisdom of the heart so that you use both sides of your brain to access your divine essence. The heart-mind connection enables us to raise our consciousness level and tune in to the Akashic Realm.

What does "a dimension of consciousness" mean? Consciousness, quite simply, is awareness. Our brain handles all kinds of amazing tasks in ways that scientists do not fully understand. For example, the brain has different regions for different functions, like memory, logic, language, art, emotion, etc. We know that we think, feel, take in information from different places, integrate what we learn, and then apply it to something new. That, my friend, is consciousness at work in a dimension that is invisible to our physical eyes. It works but we can't see it or touch it.

You might wonder, as I did, how, if the Akashic field is not a person, it can have consciousness, and from where that consciousness arises. It comes from you, me, your friends, your neighbors, your postman, your parents, your grandparents, all of your ancestors from all planets, the cats, the dogs, the squirrels, trees, houses, mountains, and land. Yes, it comes from everywhere and everyone, including the source, the divine, because each one of us is an expression of the divine source. Therefore this Universal consciousness of the Akashic Records is our connection to the source, the divine. When we tune in to it consciously, we are tuning in to the divine source of all things.

To go back to our library analogy, your Akashic Records are books on the shelf. When there is a particular question you have (challenges in your life), the answer (information) is in a particular book. You check the library computer and find the book (consciously tune in to the Universal consciousness with a tool or a key). You go to the book-shelf with the goal (intention) to find the book and get it (heart-mind connection accompanied by consciousness movement energy).

To help you learn more about how to raise your consciousness level and further your Akashic journey, I'm offering a free video series called Unlock the Door for readers of this book. You can sign up to receive it at www.akashicrecordskey.com.

CHAPTER TWO

HOW CAN THE AKASHIC RECORDS HELP YOU?

Practical Benefits of Connecting with Your Records

Remember how your soul grows from all experiences in life? If the thought of riding the roller coaster of life makes you want to shut your eyes, know that your Akashic Records is your trustworthy guide mobilized by your soul. How do you feel knowing that you do not have to go through life blindly?

Some clients have told me that they lost sleep before getting Akashic Records advice for the first time. When I asked why, they said, "I am afraid that my soul is not going to be happy with some of the things I did." Or, "I was anxious about whether the Records are going to tell me bad news." Or, "I don't know if I want to hear the truth."

Relax! Nothing bad is going to happen. Your soul knows you the best. It knows exactly what you are going through and why you did what you did. Your soul loves you so much and that is why it picked you.

The Universal Light Beings that your soul works with in the Records know exactly the information that is most beneficial for you to receive at any given time and communicate it to you. Only the relevant information that you need right now, when you are ready to receive, will be revealed to you. The depth of information you receive also depends on your relationship with your Records.

It is important to understand though, that the Records do not tell us what to do. Rather, the Records show us the truth behind a given situation; it's up to us to decide what to do.

Nancy came to me for advice. She was frustrated with her job because a more inexperienced person got the promotion she felt she should have been given years ago. After hearing that she was upset, her boss then promised her that she would be promoted in a year.

Nancy put it this way to the Records: "I do not think my boss is going to keep the promise. I have been at the job for so many years. He would have promoted me already by now. What can I do to make sure that I get this promotion I deserve?"

The Records asked, "What did your boss say you have to do to get the promotion?"

"I will have to work extra hours to prove that I deserve it," Nancy said.

"The truth is that your boss is helping you by not promoting you." said the Records.

"What?" Nancy blurted.

The Records continued, "Not only do you have to work extra hours before promotion, so will you after. Do you really want to stay late in the office or bring work home on a regular basis and not be able to spend time with your family?"

"No, I don't, actually," Nancy said. "I'm burnt out already after all those years of long hours. But I deserve it after working hard for so many years. I didn't ask for a promotion when I worked really hard and now I've missed the chance!"

"Why didn't you ask for a promotion before?" asked the Records.

"I thought if I worked hard, people would notice without me asking for it," said Nancy.

The Records asked, "How does it make you feel if you need to ask for something you deserve?"

"I feel like I am begging. It makes me very uncomfortable. I don't know. I just can't. . . ." Nancy squeezed her hands together nervously.

This conversation with Nancy's Records helped her to see that the true issue behind her promotion problem was the fact that she could not speak up for herself, which resulted from many past life experiences. Learning about these past life experiences and why she could not speak up brought Nancy a sense of relief and newfound hope. Nancy's Records then suggested she incorporate some self-care activities to improve her self-esteem and balance past-life karmas.

Nancy could have ignored the advice from her Records and continued to be the same way she had always been. Or Nancy could have taken her Record's suggestion to heart and begun taking care of herself, increasing her self-confidence and eventually learning to speak up for herself. It was her choice.

I am glad to share that Nancy chose the latter. Overtime, she felt more empowered and stopped taking a hit from people. Six months later, she was able to speak up for herself when a manager tried to blame her for a hot-potato issue that the company was trying to solve. This outcome would have been very different had Nancy been unable to stand in her power. Instead, she was able to safeguard her integrity and gain respect.

Nancy's story is just one of many examples of how your Records can help you in your career, relationship, finances, health, decision-making, and more. In addition to asking for guidance from your Records, you can also do things in your Records to deepen the experience. It is not for everyone, but when drawn to do so, people have gotten great results when doing meditation, healing, or creativity work in their Records.

Spiritual Benefit: Unlock the Utmost Potential of Your Soul's Growth

As you move along the journey, ponder all aspects in life, and make the best decisions you can with the help from your Records, you get to know yourself better by reconnecting with your own soul and its wisdom throughout all lifetimes.

You become wiser, calmer, grounded, and more emotionally collected during all the twists and turns in life, because you remember who you truly are: a spiritual being having a physical experience on Earth.

You understand that life is just an experience to raise your awareness of that. You continue to learn from all the experiences on Earth so that you can be successful moving on to the next phase of your journey!

To speed up the learning curve, our souls usually add a few spices of chaos in life.

On May 26, 2016, a little after 4am, I was woken by an electrical, arcing noise that sounded far away, but very clear. The power went out a few seconds later. I grabbed a flashlight, went to the basement, and saw the service panel popping with a glowing yellow light. 911 told me to get out of the house immediately, and that was what I did.

While I waited outside, the fire went from the basement to the first floor through the wall. Watching in disbelief as my study was devoured by the flames, many thoughts went through my mind. Desperately, I connected with my Akashic Records and asked the Light Beings to help me keep my sanity. All I could do was suspend my thoughts on why this was happening and what was going to happen next. It was like watching a movie, but it was happening to me for real.

During the first couple of days after the fire, I was in shock. My ability to focus, comprehend, and communicate deteriorated even though I was still functioning.

My study was where I planned, strategized, wrote, and dreamed. Some of the most inspiring and sentimental items were on the desk. They were all destroyed. While I understood intellectually that it was "just" a picture of my father, a clock engraved with his name, and a mug from my stepdaughter and her husband for Mother's Day, emotionally I still hurt.

After settling down in a hotel, I needed to write down all the different tasks to handle. I reached for my planner and remembered that my planner had been burned in the fire. In that moment, reality kicked in, and, heart aching, I began sobbing. What I was really crying about was that it felt like my hope was gone.

Three days after the fire, I spent some time with myself. Starting with using the sound of my voice to release trauma in my Akashic Records, I set the intention to bring me to a time where I could find the strength to get through the tragedy. I then asked my Records to help me understand why the fire happened and what I could learn from the experience. I ended the self-care with asking the Light Beings to help me release chaotic emotions.

My emotions were too high, to say the least, to understand much information from my Akashic Records in the first session. What I received was great comfort and understanding. It felt like the Light Beings in my Records knew what I was going through. They kept telling me that it was going to be all right. They still do. At the time of writing this book, I am going through a formal appraisal process for fire damage, which means I probably won't be able to move back to the house until more than a year after the fire.

How do I manage all this?

My work in the Records has been instrumental in guiding me to allow time for my emotions to process internally and to not let raw emotions spill all over or continue further into a downward spiral. The love, wisdom, support, and comfort from the Light Beings helped me to recover, accept, and eventually become emotionally grounded once again.

The Records then helped me to step back and observe my own emotions. How did I react or behave because of my emotions? What did my emotions do for me? It helped me to understand that if I want to make a difference in the world, I need to hold myself to a much higher level of emotional maturity. It helped me to see that clarity comes after detaching from the outcome of any situation.

Many people have sensed that our planet Earth is going through more and more rapid changes in all aspects--economics, environment, politics etc., both manmade and not. It is not only on a global scale but also in our immediate surroundings. Nurturing our ability to function in a world of chaos becomes critical to better managing these rapid shifts.

The Akashic Records help us to develop the skill of lifting ourselves up beyond immediate human emotions so that we can regain clarity in any turmoil. This is the key to unlocking the utmost potential of our soul's growth.

Goal: Understand that Living Your Life Is Your Highest Purpose

Some people have had a good life and some have had a tough life. Some endure physical illness or limitation. Some have financial difficulties. Some were traumatized physically, mentally, or emotionally. Some just feel that they do not belong here on Earth. Sometimes people just think that life is flat-out unfair. There is such a wide spectrum of different encounters and experiences that while many of us plow through challenges and obstacles, others want to disappear or escape from life.

The truth is that you are here on Earth because you have a job to do. Every single one of us has a place and purpose on Earth. Our souls have agreed to live on Earth not only for individual soul evolution, but also for our collective soul group development.

Almost every one of us wants to know our purpose in life. The tricky part is that just because we all have a purpose in life does not mean that it is for us to find out. Do you really know your purpose in life?

Now let's think about this. Your soul incarnated because it wants to learn as much as it is humanly possible to do. So why put a cap on that and set a limit on your potential?

Once you know your purpose, it is like you have a target. You begin chasing it and become attached to the outcome of whether you are getting there or not. Attaching to a particular outcome is limiting what other greater things you can accomplish.

Besides, free will is one of the privileges that we have as human beings. Each minute, all the future possibilities change as we make a decision and take an action. Everything is constantly changing depending on your choices from moment to moment.

What if your purpose seems so far out of reach, so ridiculously impossible, that if you heard it right now you simply would reject it and run? There is no benefit of knowing it then, is there?

Therefore, the route to finding your true purpose is simply to follow the divine guidance one step at a time and live your life. Detach from outcomes and allow all things to unfold.

This is particularly important for "star seeds" who are reincarnated on Earth. For the purposes of this book, star seeds are people whose home planets were not Earth when their souls first begin incarnation. Star seeds are souls whose original home planet was in other star systems or from other galaxies.

Star seed is a term often used in metaphysics regarding ascension. Star seeds are human beings like you and everybody else on Earth. It is critical, however, for star seeds to awaken to their souls' origin so they can reconnect with their wisdom and gifts in order to fulfill their souls' divine mission in this lifetime. Some people know they are star seeds by getting signs and clues from their spiritual searching, or by having some light bulb moments, or receiving messages from healing sessions or other spiritual practices. The Records can help provide more answers.

Before they fully awaken to their lineage, some star seed souls feel lost and not able to adapt to Earth realm vibrations. Chaos is often a divine intervention to help star seeds become aware that only when we master life on Earth will our souls learn and grow, even for star seeds. And it is only when we are fully grounded that we can bring more Light to Earth.

Just Do It! Open Records Exercise #2 – Self

Again, the purpose of this exercise is to dip your toe in the water without being overwhelmed by information or any expectation. We will go over detailed instructions later in the book.

- Have the Universal Akashic Prayer© from the beginning of the book handy.

- Read the prayer once out loud.

- Set the intention that you would like to access your own Akashic Records.

- Visualize the light of your Akashic Records coming down from your eighth chakra (approximately at arm's length when you raise your arms over your head) to your heart.

- It connects your heart to your will at the solar plexus area (below your heart and above your belly button). It then connects your heart to the divine (above your eighth chakra).

- Use your imagination or in your mind's eye (in the middle of your brow) to observe your surroundings. Notice them and let them go.

- Ask the Universal Light Beings to show you their presence in any way that you could notice. You can ask this in your mind or say it out loud if it helps you.

- Observe and let it go.

- Stay in your Records for about three minutes.

- Express gratitude to the Universal Light Beings. Say, "We are complete" out loud to end the exercise.

- Write down whatever your experience was.

How Does the Healing Happen?

The Akashic Records contain love, wisdom, and truth – all of which facilitate healings.

I asked the Akashic Records how the healing happens in this Akashic dimension. They showed me a crying baby being enveloped and comforted by a gentle tree branch. Acceptance and unconditional love supports the baby as the tree branch lifts the baby up. The baby grows stronger and taller.

Love is the healing energy. It reminds you that your soul has chosen you because you are the one and only. It shows you that you are perfect just the way you are. There is nothing broken or that needs to be fixed.

Being loved unconditionally by the divine source softens all the criticism that you cast upon yourself. It helps you to release self-judgment. Self-care becomes so much easier because you know that you are worth it. You understand that only when you can accept and love yourself first, so will your capacity to accept and love others expand.

Little by little, as healing happens, pure white light from the divine source flows in and replaces the dark cloud in your subtle energy body. Your divine essence shines brighter as you grow stronger and taller. With trust, you open your heart to see the true essence in you. The true essence that your soul has always known from its blueprint of perfection before being covered up by any experience in life.

Synchronicity occurs to inspire you with many enlightening moments and help you uncover what is truly important to you. Through that, you follow what brings your heart genuine joy.

Your heart is where your soul resides. When your heart is being nurtured by love and joy, your connection with your soul is strengthened. You hear inner guidance more clearly, and as a result, your connection with the divine becomes stronger.

Three Steps of Healing

Healing in this Akashic realm is activated by intention because intention is the heart-mind connection that gets the energy moving and enables us to raise the consciousness level and tune in to Akasha.

Energy is the movement of consciousness. It brings love, acceptance, and support into your subtle energy body. Once recognized by your energy field, the high vibration emanating from love and acceptance break down the lower vibration energy in your field so it falls away. This is the first step of healing in the Akashic Records.

When you access the Akashic Records consciously, you are asking to connect with a higher dimension of consciousness. The more you connect, the higher your consciousness level is raised. Since consciousness is awareness, you will start noticing things that you did not notice before. You will have aha moments that bring up new awareness and understanding. You will discover that things that used to be important to you are no longer important, or things that used to bother you before stop bothering you now. All of which are attributes of new perspectives inherited in the higher consciousness level. This is the second step of healing in the Akashic Records.

Information from the Records satisfies the need of your human self to process and understand, which in turn assists in the further integration of changes as they occur. This is the third step of healing in the Akashic Records.

Layers of Healing

Truth and love heal. But no healing can be completed in one single experience, as there is no magical experience that can encompass all aspects of life. Healing that results in permanent, life-changing transformation happens over time, revealing itself in layer after layer, each time going deeper toward the core.

Sometimes the wound is so deep that it takes a long time to go through layers of healing, depending on our readiness. It's like peeling a scab off the skin prematurely; it will not help, and will even delay the healing. Therefore, we often encounter the same issues that we thought we had already dealt with in different forms, and we get frustrated by our belief that no progress was made.

Know that you did overcome at the level and to the degree that you were ready to handle. Each time the wound resurfaces, you move on to the next level of healing. As you release whatever no longer serves you, you dig deeper and heal more completely. You are always moving forward on your soul's journey.

There will be times that you are not ready to take actions or make a change. That is okay. Just keep the suggestion and information from your Records in the back of your mind. If you could not do it now or even disagree with it, think about the reasons and write them down. Then explore the same topic next time you are ready to give it another try.

Keeping note of reasons why you could not do it will help you sort through hidden issues. Then you can explore the truth behind the "whys" in the Records should you decide to do so.

CHAPTER THREE

THE UNIVERSAL AKASHIC PRAYER© (UAP)

Different Prayers for Different People

There are many different prayers to access the Akashic Records. Some are published and some are kept private. All of them exist because they are needed.

There are infinite dimensions in the Akashic Records. Each dimension has its unique range of vibration. Each word has its vibration and hence, each prayer has its own unique vibration level that can access information in the same vibrational dimension of the Records. Your own consciousness level also affects the level of dimension you can tune in to in the Records.

Each one of us is a unique individual, each at a different stage of our journey and with different needs. What works best for our needs now is the prayer that will come across for us to use. This is one of many reasons for various prayers.

As you change by stepping forward on the path of personal growth, what resonates with you will change as well. This is a good thing, and a sign that you're paying attention to the internal shifts that will lead you to the next phase of your journey. This is another reason for the existence of many prayers.

Your connection to your first few home planets also has deep impact on which prayer works the best for you because that connection holds the key to help you adapt to the Earth vibration so that your soul can reach the highest potential here.

Your relationship with your Akashic Records is yet another important factor in what vibration of the prayer may work best for you. The stronger the relationship, the higher vibrational dimension you will reach in the Records. Hence a prayer that can support the work in that vibrational level or higher will be needed.

What it comes down to is what feels the most natural to you. This depends on where your soul's origin is, the first few home planets of incarnation, your consciousness level, your relationship with your Akashic Records, and where you are on your journey.

Needless to say, there is no one-size-fits-all prayer.

It is not unusual to find, after you've worked with a prayer for a while and built a strong relationship with your Records, that you can access the Records with intention alone and don't need to read the prayer. That is because your consciousness has mastered shifting between the 3D dimensions on Earth and that particular higher dimension in the Records.

Then, if you want to access the next higher level dimension in the Records, you will need a new prayer that can lead you there. This observation is based on my own experience as well as that of my peers and my students.

That's why I started with the first prayer I learned to access the Records, later found myself resonate more with the second prayer shared with me, and am now using the third prayer given to me by the Records. I will not be surprised by more new prayers given by the Records as we collectively continue to grow and ready ourselves for higher dimensions.

Where Did It Come From?

Before I share how the prayer came about, I have to tell you about my soul friend and best friend, Lynne Grobsky. Without her help, I would not be writing this book or sharing this prayer with you.

Lynne and I met in the spring of 2014 through Linda Howe's online Akashic Records Teacher training program.

We found out that we both live in Connecticut by the area code of our phone numbers when we were assigned as reading partners for one of the homework exercises. I was puzzled and asked the Universe "WHY?" when I realized that there was another person in the same class in Connecticut. You see, I wanted to be the only one to teach this cool class locally.

Little did I know back then that this was all part of the Universal plan. Lynne and I live only 20 minutes apart for a reason. Our souls agreed to help each other on the spiritual journey in this lifetime! Looking back, I understand now that my resistance of another person teaching the same class locally was coming from my non-integrated ego which we will talk more later in the book.

Since we live so close to each other, we decided to be reading partners after we became certified teachers. Back then, there were many issues that were just too close to home for me to get a clear picture, so I looked to Lynne's help to get confirmation and information from my Records during our routine Akashic Records exchange. That is exactly how the Universal Akashic Prayer© came about.

In the planning stages of this book, I was thrilled that Fran, the founder of The Akashic Network and receiver of the Akashic Access Prayer©, gave me permission to use that prayer as well as the TAN curriculum to write this book. But as I began mapping the outline and structure of the book, I ran into major roadblocks.

It was extremely difficult for me to figure out how I was going to use the Akashic Access Prayer© and the TAN curriculum and still freely write what I wanted to write. Integrity and honesty are the two things that I pride myself with. If I were to write this book based on TAN's work, I would definitely make sure the content of the book followed it.

However, I had this weird but strong feeling that something was not right. I didn't know why, but I felt limited, as if my hands were tied—and there seemed to be no reason, since Fran gave me full-range freedom to write using TAN's work.

The question of what future courses should be based on this book also tore me apart. There was a sense of knowing that future courses based on this book would not be the same as TAN's curriculum. I had no idea why I had all these misgivings or where they came from. I was so lost and stuck, and I couldn't see how to move forward. Then the question of whether I needed a new prayer for teaching crossed my mind.

On October 24, 2016, during our routine exchange, I explored the issues that I was having. I sought guidance from my Records, through Lynne, on the most efficient way to write this book and appropriate content for the book.

Even though I knew the Records were not going to bite me, so to speak, my stomach felt like it was in my throat as I asked the question, "So is it still efficient to use the Akashic

Access Prayer©? There is no need for me to ask for my own prayer for this book?"

I held my breath as I watched Lynne, eyes closed, talking to my Records. She said, "How accurate is the statement that Jiayuh would benefit from using the current prayer and not her own?" Lynne was made to understand that the statement was 80% accurate.

Given that Lynne is so skillful and experienced with the Akashic Records, she went on to ask, "So what will be the effect of Jiayuh asking for a different prayer?" Upon hearing that, my entire body jerked from my chair and leaned forward in anticipation as my Records showed Lynne a visual image of fireworks for a different prayer. For Lynne, the image of fireworks is a way the Records communicate a positive impact to her.

My voice cranked up involuntarily and I shouted in disbelief, "What? Seriously? Why?"

My Records replied, "Because this is going to be the core of your book, of your certification, a new prayer." Lynne was shivering and getting goose bumps as she verified from my Records that this statement was 100% accurate with a visual confirmation of an image of fireworks.

All I could do was stare at Lynne tearing up as she felt the tremendous impact of the new prayer and confirmation from my Records that it was time for me to get my own prayer. Lynne's reaction solidified the truth in my mind, and that is when I burst into tears, too. Lynne went on to verify information about the timing of receiving the new prayer and her part in helping me get the new prayer transmitted from the Records. I didn't know what to think.

The air was filled with Lynne's conversation with my Records as well as my uncontrollable sobbing. There were so many mixed and complicated emotions, as if there was a little kitten playing with balls of yarn, all messily intertwined, in my head.

I flashed back to images of the five of us – Fran, Gwendolyn, Laura, Lynne and me – having discussion after discussion on how to share the Akashic Access Prayer© with the world, and of some of us having to build our Akashic Records career all over again with a new curriculum after stopping teaching Linda's program. The thought of doing something like that yet again, this time on my own, was so heavy that I could not see myself through it.

And yet, the Records comforted me that I was not alone in this. They verified that a new prayer needed to come through for this book and that this was exactly why I had such a difficult time trying to figure out how to use the Akashic Access Prayer© and the TAN curriculum in my book. Additionally, the Records confirmed that one of the reasons that the new prayer would be able to come through me was because I had honored my soul's wisdom when I reclaimed my birth name earlier that year.

All these validations and confirmations were powerful, but my fears simply would not go away. Still in tears, voice cracking, I asked one more time, "Are they *sure* that I am supposed to have a prayer?"

Lynne received the knowing from my Records: "That is your non-integrated ego. And yes, that is 100% accurate. Why are you not fine with it?"

I struggled to form a complete sentence because I was out of breath from crying. I said, "Because it is scary . . . to fight again. I am not strong enough. . . . It is scary because I saw the challenges that Fran had to go through when she had a new prayer." Then I started mumbling, "I don't know if the new prayer will work. . . ."

Lynne patiently waited for me to stop crying, then delivered the final message from the Records. "Fran did not have the support you have. She came through with what was needed at the time to get us boosted, to get us going. This is the next step in bringing the Akashic Light to the world. So you are not alone. This is not yours alone. You have support. This is part of our sacred contract. This is part of Angela's (my mentor and publisher's) sacred contract in bringing a new level of Akashic Light into the world. But it is not you. It is a collaborative effort."

It took me a while to process all this. I thought, "I am just me. Who am I to receive a new prayer?" My self-doubt and fears stirred deep inside me as I cried for another day after the exchange.

Then I realized that a new prayer only comes through in a time it is needed. I did and do believe there are people who have been waiting for information that's to be brought through with this new prayer. I also knew that I was not the only candidate. If I was not willing to bring this new prayer through, the Records would find somebody else to do the job. It was up to my free will.

It brought me a sense of pride to know that I was chosen as a candidate for my soul's wisdom when I reclaimed my birth name. So who did I want to be? I wanted to be the person who steps up above human fears and is of service to mankind. Then I sat in my Records and told the Records that I was willing to accept the job.

On October 30, 2016, during our next routine Akashic Records exchange, the Records gave us the first three lines of the prayer while Lynne was in my Records. I could not help but use that three-line partial prayer to open Lynne's Records next. As soon as I finished saying the first three lines, the Records gave us the last three lines. Together, we received this new prayer from the Records:

The Universal Akashic Prayer© (UAP)

Dear Universal Light Beings,

We hold your love, light, and wisdom in our hearts.

Please help us to be a clear channel with complete trust

in our ability to surrender our human judgment.

Please help us to connect with open hearts,

And to know the truth of our existence.

So that we may be of service for the highest good of all.

Instruction to Open the Akashic Records

If you are new to the Akashic Records or not confident in your work with the Records, preparing yourself for a shift in consciousness will help. A meditation connecting with the Mother Earth and the Divine Source is good for preparing. For readers of this book, I have created a Light Meditation recording in my Unlock the Door video series free as my gift to you. You can sign up for it at www.akashi-crecordskey.com.

Read the prayer out loud once.

If you are totally new to the Akashic Records and find yourself wondering whether you are in the Records or not, know that you absolutely are. However, if it makes you feel more confident, you can read the prayer out loud a second time before you move on to the next step.

After reading the six-line prayer no more than two times, set the intention that you would like to access your own Akashic Records. Just think in your own head "I would like to access my Akashic Records." There is no need to state this intention out loud. Remember the intention, and not the specific name, makes the consciousness move. Therefore, a first name to help you focus your intention on a particular person in your mind is sufficient if you are doing this for others. If you are doing it for a non-human, use the way you call that non-human to help you focus and set the intention. You will see how that's done later in the book.

Once the intention to access the Akashic Records is set, feel the light connection from heart to solar plexus and from heart to divine. Visualize the light of your Akashic Records coming down from your eighth chakra (approximately at arm's length when you raise your arms above your head) to your heart. It connects your heart to your will at the solar plexus area (below your heart and above your belly button). It then connects your heart to the divine (above your eighth chakra). The divine light might be strong and travel to your root chakra at the base of your spine. Know that it is fine however it unfolds. Everyone's experience is different.

Instruction to Close the Akashic Records

At the end of the reading, ask the client if she/he feels complete (or ask yourself if you open your own Records). If yes, thank the Divine Source and Light Beings with deep gratitude for their help and say, "We are complete" out loud to close the Records and end the reading.

Just Do It! Open Records Exercise #3 – Self

The purpose of Exercise #3 is to establish a baseline so that later on you can see the progress when you do the same exercise again.

There are two parts to this exercise. Pick one question you would like to explore and ask the same question in two different ways so you can compare and contrast. Part one is getting the answer from your heart. Part two is getting the answer from your Records.

PART ONE – FROM YOUR HEART AND OUTSIDE OF YOUR RECORDS

1. Set the intention to connect with your heart.

2. Ask your heart the question. You can say it either silently in your mind or out loud.

3. Give it five minutes to allow information to flow to you.

4. Write down what you get from your heart.

PART TWO – IN YOUR RECORDS

Have the Universal Akashic Prayer© handy.

Open the Records:

1. Read the prayer once out loud. You can read it twice out loud if you feel the need.

2. Set the intention that you would like to access your own Akashic Records.

3. Visualize the light of your Akashic Records coming down from your eighth chakra (approximately at arm's length when you raise your arms above your head) to

your heart. It connects your heart to your will at the solar plexus area (below your heart and above your belly button). It then connects your heart to the divine (above your eighth chakra).

4. Use your imagination or in your mind's eye (in the middle of your brow) to observe your surroundings. Notice them and let them go.

5. Ask the Universal Light Beings to show you their presence in any way that you could notice. Observe and let it go.

Ask your questions in the Records:

6. Ask your Records the same question as in Part One. Ask the Universal Light Beings to communicate with you in any way that you would understand.

7. Stay in your Records for five minutes.

Close Records:

8. Express gratitude to the Universal Light Beings. Say "We are complete." out loud to end the exercise.

9. Write down whatever you get in the Records.

BONUS PART THREE – IN YOUR RECORDS

Have the Universal Akashic Prayer© handy.

Open Records:

1. Read the prayer once out loud. You can read it twice out loud if you feel the need.

2. Set the intention that you would like to access your own Akashic Records.

3. Visualize the light of your Akashic Records coming down from your eighth chakra (approximately at arm's length when you raise your arms above your head) to your heart. It connects your heart to your will at the solar plexus area (below your heart and above your belly button). It then connects your heart to the divine (above your eighth chakra).

4. Use your inner eye (your third eye in the middle of the brow) to observe your surroundings. Notice them and let them go.

5. Ask the Universal Light Beings to show you their presence in any way that you could notice. Observe and let it go

Ask your questions:

6. Ask your Records, "What is the difference between the two methods, connecting with your heart vs. connecting with your Records?" Ask the Universal Light Beings to communicate with you in any way that you would understand.

7. Stay in your Records for five minutes.

Close Records:

8. Express gratitude to the Universal Light Beings. Say, "We are complete" out loud to end the exercise.

9. Write down whatever you get in the Records.

In the Three Steps of Healing section, we talked about that healing in this Akashic Realm is activated by intention because intention is the heart-mind connection to get the energy moving and enables us to raise the consciousness level and tune in to Akasha. We also discussed, in How Does the Healing Happen? section, that your heart is where your soul resides. Working in the Records strengthens the connection between your heart and soul and, hence, the divine. Overtime, you will find these two methods converge since your heart connection with the divine becomes stronger and stays connected even in an ordinary state.

What Are These Words and Why?

In the Universal Akashic Prayer©, "we" is used because each time a person opens the Records with this prayer it is on behalf of all the people in the soul group at the same vibration on the same path.

In the second line, the words "love" and "light" are used for healing. The word "wisdom" represents insights and information. All three are to be held in our hearts to facilitate transformation.

The third line of the prayer is to bring in trust in the divine so that we can release our judgment and get ourselves out of the way.

The forth line is to receive the divine guidance with an open heart.

The fifth line is to ask for the truth.

The sixth line is the intention of receiving truth to serve for the highest good of all in the soul group.

Uniqueness of the Universal Akashic Prayer©

The first time I used the Universal Akashic Prayer© to read Lynne, I had goose bumps all over my body with every line I read. That is how I knew the vibration of this prayer is higher than the ones I used before. With my mind's eye, I saw I was standing in a place with a cloud-like ocean of light. All of the Light Beings were right there closely around me instead of being high above me or far away. They were not the same Light Beings I had worked with before. I could feel that we had accessed a higher dimension, a different realm, in the Records.

Three weeks later, Lynne shared with me some feedback from a student, Jack, with whom she had used the Universal Akashic Prayer© for a support coaching session. Previously, she had taught with Jack the TAN curriculum using the Akashic Access Prayer©. In this particular coaching session, Jack opened his own Records using the Akashic Access Prayer© while Lynne opened Jack's Records with the Universal Akashic Prayer©. Jack reported that he saw the ocean of light above him with Light Beings there who are not the same Light Beings he works with using the Akashic Access Prayer©. He knew he was not ready to use the new prayer, but he felt that he was getting closer.

This prayer opens up the Akashic Records at the collective soul level. Every time a person opens their own Records they are bringing information and transformation back to the entire soul group. The group consciousness level is much stronger and more coherent than the level I connected with before. The Records want us to understand the uniqueness of the prayer. That is why "we" is used in the prayer, and also why Lynne and I received the prayer together.

Upon further inquiry, the Records let us know that the Universal Akashic Prayer© connects to the dimension of Universal view and truth in the Records, and therefore information about star lineage and galactic levels will be revealed when it is relevant to the matters at hand.

Intention is the way to communicate in the dimensions accessed through this prayer. Intention moves the energy and gets the energy going in the Records, as well as facilitates healing. Therefore, there is no need to verbalize a name for opening the Records or specify an exact legal name or full address for the Records you would like to access. All you need to do is to set intention for all that without the need to specify details.

For the same reason, there is no need to announce, "The Records are now open," as is the case using other prayers.

It's also not necessary to read a closing prayer or announce, "The Records are now closed." Intention at work contributes to the high vibration and effectiveness of this simple and short prayer.

Please know that this prayer is not for everyone. Earlier in this book, we discussed how each one of us resonates with different vibration and prayer at any given time on the journey. I am very grateful, however, that the Universal view and truth can be shared through this prayer because I know there are people who are ready for the information now just as I am.

Light Beings Who Work with You

The Light Beings in this realm of the Records are not just earthbound ones. Different Universal Light Beings from various star systems can step forward and communicate information depending on what is needed at the time. For star seeds, these Light Beings include those who worked with your soul during lifetimes on different planets. If group consciousness is the foundation of the non-Earth planets that your soul incarnated on, then these Universal Light Beings would work together in a similar way.

As I understand it, a soul could have lifetimes in many different star systems. Therefore, what support needed from which star system could vary depending on what is most relevant to a soul's current experience on Earth.

At the time of writing this book, these Light Beings do not seem to have specific names or titles. They do not seem to care about those. In my mind's eye, they simply smile nicely at me when I ask about it, as if it is not important to them.

The higher the level we are within the Akasha, the more Light Beings there are. Because of the high vibration, they are all working together like in an orchestra. The roles are very subtle and interchangeable. Trying to assign roles and names lowers the vibration. Another point they make is that all the Light Beings step in and out just as fast as the person evolves to a higher realm. Therefore, it is a moot point to have names.

Can You Get a Prayer for Yourself?

Yes, I do believe so. New prayers could be gifted to human race by the Akashic Records if there is a need from the Record's perspective.

The question is whether you have established a strong working relationship with your Akashic Records to help you get yourself out of the way so that you can have clarity in the Akashic Records on whether the prayer is given to you by the Records or created by your human self from your non-integrated ego. Therefore, an integrated ego that has reached the state of detaching from all outcomes is one of the requirements to be able to receive a new prayer from the Records. We will talk about integrated and non-integrated ego later in the book.

A strong relationship with your Records also helps you test the vibration level of the prayer. The relationship with your Records is built on spending time with your Records, increasing communication, following the guidance, and more, which we will discuss later in the book.

From the Records' viewpoint, it would give out new prayers when there is a need for the human race to take the next step and reach a higher degree of development.

Can You Change the Words of the Prayer?

Words in the prayer are given by the Akashic Records so that it can be truly understood by a person and lead them to the higher dimension level by resonance. Just as a new prayer, changing words in a prayer can also be given by the Akashic Records. Most likely it becomes a new prayer and is given to be shared with the public. At a human-self personal level, whether you can change words of the prayer depends on your consciousness level. If your consciousness level is there, words won't matter because you are there already with intention. This is why, over time, it is possible to get to a particular level of the Akasha with pure intention and without a prayer. Conversely, if your consciousness level is not there, you will need to use the exact words of the prayer to get there.

One day, as your consciousness level rises and when you are ready to get to the next higher level, you might find yourself given words by the Akashic Records while in the

Records to get to yet another higher realm in the Akasha and to share it with the rest of the world. At that point, please remember that it is important to test the vibration of the new prayer.

As a thank you for reading this book, I'm offering my Unlock the Door video series free as my gift to you, to help you further your Akashic journey. You can sign up to receive it at www.akashicrecordskey.com.

CHAPTER FOUR

GUIDELINES TO ACCESS THE AKASHIC RECORDS

Accessing the Akashic Records is an extremely personal activity. We are talking about soul work here! It is a quest of self-discovery. It is so intimate that it requires total privacy and confidentiality. Consider it just as private as using the bathroom or taking a shower. Therefore, conscious permission is an important piece in exercising this privilege to access someone else's Records. No one should jump into the shower with someone else without a conscious invitation first. Get it?

Reading Guidelines – Self

External Substances:

Working with the Akashic Records is based on your consciousness level. So any external substance that interferes with your own consciousness level also affects the quality of your work in the Records. If alcohol, drugs, or anything that you are allergic to would prevent you from receiving clarity, you will want to wait until the effects have passed before you work with the Records.

There is one exception: anything your body truly needs in order to function. For example, prescription drugs for the purpose of maintaining your health, insulin for a diabetic, or an analgesic to stop a terrible migraine would all fall into this category and would be okay to take without interfering with your work in the Records.

How long you need to wait for the effects of other substances to dissipate depends on your own consciousness level. You can experiment yourself and see the quality of the information you receive in the Records to determine the length of time you need to be clear of the effect. You can also ask your Records for guidance.

If you are new to the Records and not experienced enough to be able to tell, you can start with waiting for 24 hours to be safe.

After you feel confident with working in the Records, you can seek guidance from there. Keep in mind, though, that the time you might need to wait after a shot of vodka versus a bottle of beer might be different.

My personal experience is that the Records guidance is typically rounded at every 4 hours, such as 24 hours, 20 hours, 16 hours, or 12 hours, but your Records' guidance for you might be different. Again, if you want to keep things simple and easy to remember, just wait 24 hours to cover everything.

Age:

One of the signature traits of working with the Records is that it does not make decisions for us. It provides insights and information, but it is up to our free will to decide the actions we want to take.

Minors who can't legally make decisions for themselves would not benefit from working with the Records, since the ultimate decisions rest with their legal guardians and not themselves. In addition, it is not the best use of the Records to get caught in the dramas created from the immature human emotions of teenagers regardless the maturity of their souls.

Do not open your own Records if you are under age 18 in the USA. For other countries, please follow local laws for what age is considered the age of consent.

Reading Guidelines – Non-human

External Substances:

Follow the same guidelines as in reading for yourself.

Permission:

Permission is required from your own pets. You can ask your dogs or cats if they want a reading. If they walk away, that means no. If they stay, that means yes. When a person comes to you for a reading of their pet's Records, make sure you instruct the owner to get their pet's permission ahead of time.

Permission is not required for an entity that is not a living being but is something that legally belongs to you, such as your own house, business, crystal, land, etc.

Permission from the owner is required for any non-living thing that is not yours.

Permission is not required for anything that is publicly accessible or known, such as national park, landmark, or public building, etc.

When in doubt, ask for guidance from your own Records as to how best to proceed.

Reading Guidelines – Other people

External Substances:

Follow the same guidelines as in reading for yourself.

Age:

Follow the same guidelines as in reading for yourself.

Permission:

Conscious permission is required. Conscious permission means the person has to give you permission while conscious and without any outside influence.

Confidentiality:

The conversation with the soul is a very personal experience. Deep healing at the conscious level occurs when connecting with the Akashic Records. It requires no distraction from other people. Therefore, no third party should be present in a live session.

Even though a client might ask to have their parents, best friends, or soul mate be present for moral support, they can't be in the same room with the client listening to the conversation with the client's own soul.

As an Akashic Records advisor, you need to understand that we never know what the client's Records are going to reveal. Sometimes, it is not in your client's best interest for anybody else to hear certain new information.

CHAPTER FIVE

ACCESS THE AKASHIC RECORDS FOR YOURSELF

Before you start, please review Chapter 3 on the prayer instruction and Chapter 4 on the guidelines.

Your Soul Has Your Best Interests in Mind

It is important to understand that connecting with your soul's wisdom is not the same as a psychic reading or past life regression. You are not channeling information from external sources. Rather, you are reaching within yourself for insights that you already possess, but are disconnected from until now.

Remember that you are the perfect person who your soul has chosen for its journey because of everything you will learn from experiences in life.

We all know that the highest form of learning does not come from following orders. Instead, it comes from understanding, inspiration, and awareness, and that is exactly what your soul wishes for you on your journey in life. After all, your soul is your teammate who has your best interests in mind!

For this reason, you get to exercise the unique gift of free will as a human being and decide the actions you are going to take. Therefore, the job of your soul is to provide you with all the information you need to make the best choice for the next step.

It's not unusual for us to feel that there are some things that we want to hear about more than others and other things we don't want to know about at all. So it does happen at times that whatever we are seeking information about is not always what we need. In those instances, our souls may provide information we don't want to hear but that is necessary in order for us to move on.

When that happens, it is usually because it is very important for you to be aware of this particular truth and face it for your highest and best good. It is like a spiritual growing pain – unpleasant but necessary. Look beyond the temporary feeling of being uncomfortable. Do your best to follow the guidance of your Records. And get ready for the big shift coming up. You will be glad you did when you look back!

Hmm, why do I feel that the above is so familiar? Ahh, duh . . . that is how I got the Universal Akashic Prayer©. Have to laugh!

Communicate with Your Records

Note the word "communicate" with your Records.

Think about all the relationships you have had. What did you do when you meet a person for the first time? You talk to get to know each other.

Would you ask for a large personal loan from a stranger who is in line with you to get coffee? Would you ask someone to marry you on the first date? Probably not.

Your Akashic Records is in a way like a long lost, super-smart aspect of yourself that you just found out about. Therefore, it's critical to build a relationship through spending time together, having conversations, and getting to know each other in order to get comfortable and get the best quality information you can from your Records.

When you open a dialogue with your Records, you'll want to be specific about what you seek to know more about. The words you use help find information that matches more precisely with the experience you want to explore. Very much like typing in the right key words for Googling a subject in a cyber sea of information.

The nature of the question dictates the answers. Tapping into your soul's wisdom is not for curiosity, entertainment, showing off, prediction, speculation, or avoiding having to make your own decisions. Therefore, those kinds of questions would not get much response, if any, from your Records. Through practice, you will learn a better way to ask questions.

You will want to describe the situation, state how you feel about the situation, and state what you want to know. It is better to be specific. Only the information that is relevant for the matters at hand in your life right now and for whatever learning will help you navigate through challenge will be revealed. After you receive the information from the Records, you can ask the Records about accuracy to confirm.

The way you communicate with your Records changes over time as your relationship grows stronger. A strong relationship with your Records enhances the heart-mind connection that is the ability to raise the consciousness level in the Records. The higher your consciousness level is, the easier it is to communicate with your Records, since you can tune in to the Records more easily.

Typically in the early stage of working with your Records, you will find yourself spending more time describing the situation and telling your story before sufficient information starts to flow from the Records. You probably won't get a response from the Records to your yes/no questions either.

This is because you and your Records are still new to each other and need time and practice to figure out the best way to communicate. After working with your Records consistently, as with any spiritual practice for an extended period of time, you will find that information comes through much more quickly. The need to explain a situation in detail will be lessened. Yes/no questions could possibly be answered by your Records depending on the situation.

This is because your Records have now become your best friend with whom you talk every day and share everything in your life with. And this progression is why, among other reasons, the style of my conversation with my Records through Lynne in this book about this prayer is totally different from the style in my early days working with my Records.

How does a person receive information for the Records? Everyone is different. Some people get visual images. Some hear, some feel, and some have a sense of knowing. The way you receive information is a gift to you. There is no need to compare yourself with other people, as we all have different gifts. The more you work with your Records, the more ways you will find to receive information.

Just Do It! Open Records Exercise #4 – Self

The purpose of this exercise is to help you and your Records find the best way to communicate with each other.

Take a moment to think about your learning process. What is the easiest way for you to understand things? Is it visual? Is it auditory? Is it feeling or knowing? Next, think about if you have any preference in how your Records communicate information to you. If so, write down what it is to use for this exercise. You can use an imaginary recorder to describe the information received from the Records and see if that helps you during the exercise.

Just so you don't have to page through this book to find it, here is the prayer again for you to use:

The Universal Akashic Prayer© (UAP)

Dear Universal Light Beings,

We hold your love, light, and wisdom in our hearts.

Please help us to be a clear channel with complete trust

in our ability to surrender our human judgment.

Please help us to connect with open hearts,

And to know the truth of our existence.

So that we may be of service for the highest good of all.

Open Records:

1. Read the prayer once out loud. You can read it twice out loud if you feel the need.

2. Set the intention that you would like to access your own Akashic Records. Do this in your head and do not say it out loud. However, if you are alone by yourself, you can say it out loud if it helps you.

3. Visualize the light of your Akashic Records coming down from your eighth chakra (approximately at arm's length when you raise your arms above your head) to your heart. It connects your heart to your will at the solar plexus area (below your heart and above your belly button). It then connects your heart to the divine (above your eighth chakra).

4. Use your imagination or in your mind's eye (in the middle of your brow) to observe your surroundings. Notice them and let them go.

5. In your mind, ask the Universal Light Beings to show you their presence in any way that you could notice. Observe and let it go.

Ask questions in your Records:

6. This time, say it out loud and tell your Records that you would like to find the best way for you to communicate with each other. Then go ahead and tell your Records what you think the easiest way is for you to understand things.

7. Next, say it out loud and tell your Records that you would like to understand what unconditional love is. Ask your Records to help you understand unconditional love the way that you said it is the easiest for you

to understand. Wait for three minutes for information to flow through.

8. Next, say it out loud and ask your Records to help you understand unconditional love the way that your Records think is the easiest for you to understand. Wait for 3 minutes for information to flow through.

Close Records:

9. Express gratitude to the Universal Light Beings. Say, "We are complete" out loud to end the exercise.

10. Take a moment to compare what you got from step 7 and step 8 above in the Records. Write down the method of communication in each step, your understanding of unconditional love in each method, and which method of communication help you understand better. Again, you can use an imaginary recorder and describe verbally for this if it helps you.

Are the methods from both steps 7 and 8 in the Records the same or different? Is either method from step 7 or 8 your preferred method of communication now?

You can do this exercise repeatedly with different topics to ask and help you and your Records identify the best way to communicate with each other. Instead of understanding unconditional love, you can try understanding courage, forgiveness, strength, or trust, etc.

CHAPTER SIX

IS IT REALLY FROM THE RECORDS?

Congratulations! You have come this far! The fact that you are still reading means this book resonates with you. Before you move on to learn how to access the Records for non-humans as well as other people, let's first make sure you have all the tools you need to clear the way.

So far you have done four Open Records exercises for yourself. How was your experience? Did you get some information or did you get nothing from the Records? Were you comfortable and trusting that you were in the Records? Or did you notice your mind kept thinking, "Was that from the Records or did I just make that up?"

If you fall into the former group, good for you! If you fall into the latter group along with most people, including me, welcome to the club! And don't worry, that is why this chapter exists.

The prayer and method that the Records share with us in this book are simple and straightforward. It is not easy though, to trust that it is indeed that simple and straightforward. In this chapter, I will point out some of the pitfalls that stand in the way of your confidence and the Records.

Move Human Self-Centeredness out of the Way

What exactly is self-centeredness? It includes self-importance, self-doubt, unworthiness, and much more. Basically, it is any kind of judgment you cast on yourself. Self-centeredness is the ego that has not been integrated with the divine source and gets us wound up in either direction about ourselves. An integrated ego moves us away from self-centeredness and keeps our attention clear of our human emotions, which enables us to observe ourselves and have clarity on the effect of our actions.

It is human nature to have a certain level of expectation of the experience in the Records. If you do, release it. It is very normal to assess how we perform according to our own anticipation. If you do, let go of that, too.

When we go into the Records, we do so by shifting our consciousness to a higher realm. It is a very subtle change. You are not going to see a marching band welcoming you, or thundering light representing super power in front of you. The energy of the Records is a loving and peaceful state of consciousness.

After reading the prayer and setting the intention of connecting with the Records, you are there in the Records. Remember that information is everywhere, inside and outside of all of us. Your heart and consciousness already connect to the Akasha. It is your mind that is busy analyzing and not tuning in to the information right in front of you.

Therefore, all you need to do is trust the process, know that you are in the Records, let go of judgment, and detach from the outcome. This is easy to say, but very difficult to do, as I experienced myself firsthand.

I had a great experience in my first Akashic Records class with Patty. After I went home and practiced it on my own, however, I fell flat. I got information, but it was very blurry to me. Every time I got something, I would be thinking in the back of my mind, "Is this really from the Records or did I just make that up?" It felt like the information came and went like a speed train and I could not get hold of it.

So my entire session was a repetitive loop of receiving information, then reflexively doubting, which was exactly why the information was not clear to me. In the class, I had less self-doubt because Patty's presence gave me confidence. Also, Patty was holding the space for us to have deeper connection with the Records. I did not know that until I became a teacher myself.

I went through three months of questioning, analyzing, and doubting while in the Records. One day, my mind was simply too exhausted to question anything. Then, bang! The information came through as clear as a bell. That was when I realized that my busy and analytical mind was actually preventing me from getting information clearly.

Later on, I found out from my own experience that recording my own sessions helped me a great deal to move myself out of the way. You can try this by either using an actual digital recording device or by speaking into an imaginary recorder in your hand. When your brain is engaged in describing the information, it somehow distracts your brain from wondering whether you made it up. Go ahead and redo all those exercises using a recording device and see how it works for you.

Practice, Practice, Practice

When in doubt, practice more.

The nature of the question dictates the answer. How we ask questions in the Records is very important. Asking the right question is a skill that requires practice. Further, overcoming our natural self-centeredness (non-integrated ego) takes time and practice.

The more you work with your Records, the deeper you heal, the clearer the way, the stronger the connection, and the easier the communication becomes. Work with your Records consistently, just as you do with any spiritual practice. The recommendation is at least five days a week for 15 minutes each time.

In my very early days working with my Records, I did not spend much time with it. In fact, I was so busy at work (I was still an actuary then) that I probably opened my Records twice a week at the most, which also contributed to my struggle.

It got to a point that I had to get better if I wanted to use this as a tool, so I made sure to work with my Records at least three times a week, and then five times a week. The difference it made in clarity was significant.

Some people say they do not have a question to ask the Records. You do not have to ask questions in your Records. You can just set the intention to connect and sit in the energy. You can do meditation in your Records if you would like.

Another good way to work with your Records is to map out your to-do list or run through your entire day in the Records for suggestions. You can also ask your Records to help you release anxiety, fears, or anger if you are going through some problems.

Why Does It Feel Like a Moving Target?

Another reason that people question whether information is coming from the Records is because sometimes the answer often changes for the same question. It feels like a moving target. This makes it particularly difficult for people who are new to the Records to understand what is going on.

I was frustrated when I first encountered situations like this. I trusted the information I got from the Records and acted on it, but then the advice changed next time around. Did it mean the information I got last time was not right? Should I follow this new guidance? Lots of questions went through my mind as I tried to make sense of it.

As this happened more, I began to ask my Records why the advice changed and came to understand some really cool reasons. On our journey, there are unlimited future possibilities ahead of us. Our actions determine the highest potential of a future possibility. Therefore, as we take actions, the right next step changes, and the outcome changes.

YES, the Akasha is alive.

YES, your future is yet to be written by you!

Congratulations - you have grown!

In July 2016, as I was mapping out my fall class schedule, my Records advised that it would be beneficial for me to set up local workshops. I followed the guidance and set those up. In early September of 2016, as I double checked my fall events, my Records advised that it would *not* be beneficial for me to have local workshops. Sounds confusing, right?

A few years back, I would have been freaking out and frustrated. But I knew there was a reason my Records changed the advice. I kind of figured out why at the time, but I wasn't sure until September 15, 2016.

You see, I sent in an application for The Author Incubator Idea to Done Writing Program on August 24 and the interview with Angela Lauria, President of The Author Incubator, was on September 15. If I were to get accepted into the program, I would focus on writing and not have time to facilitate workshops that fall. Well, you are reading this book. Ta-da! My Records were right on!

Availability of Star Lineage Information

We mentioned star seeds earlier in the book. It is important to recognize that the information of star lineage does not come automatically or on demand from the Records. The information is conveyed only to those who are ready to receive.

Only a solid, grounded lighthouse can shine the light for others in the storm. Issues in the Earth realm are always first priority to be overcome, since challenges are a divine intervention to help us understand that mastering life on Earth is the first step toward our soul's growth.

Therefore, star lineage information may be revealed depending on many aspects of the person inquiring: spiritual maturity, integration of the ego, consciousness level, awareness, openness. It is not the type of information you chase after out of curiosity or for bragging rights. Rather, you have to first be the person who is ready to receive the information for the greater good of all. The information is truly given to help you help others, and not for satisfying the non-integrated ego which takes time and spiritual maturity to detect.

It is also driven by divine timing. Allow the Universe to cue you with signs that it is time for you to ask and receive the information.

The way that star lineage information gets introduced in the Records varies by the stars, the person, the nature of the question, and magnitude of information. The nature of the question dictates the answer. In addition, the Light Beings will know whether you are ready to receive the information through the nature of your question.

The information could be communicated to you just like the information you receive on Earth realm issues, especially if it is a very general question such as, "What is my relationship with ABC star?" If the question is very specific, the information might need to be translated into decipherable human brain waves first, particularly if it is a big chunk of comprehensive details.

I have been working with Arcturian Healing since 2013.

The idea of working with spiritual beings from a different star system was crazy wild to me at the time. It was just a type of energy work to me.

Starting in January 2016, I was drawn strongly to work with Arcturian Healing in group settings. As I facilitated more and more group workshops, I was shown in my mind's eye that a method to work with Universal Sacred Geometry codes has been gifted to me.

That was when I was prompted to ask questions in my Records about my relationship with the Arcturian. The information was given to me the same way my Records always do, and I understood that I was an Arcturian at some point. All righty then! Since then I have become more receptive to the star seeds concept.

After my house fire, I started listening to Tom Kenyon's sound healing music every day. It brings tears to my eyes every single time. Even though I had only learned of him a short time previously, I was shocked by the impact of his music on me. I knew I had to attend his very last Hathor Intensive in Seattle in November 2016, so off I went.

It was absolutely a transformational, intense three-day workshop at the Hathor Intensive. Furthermore, I was shown that another form of energy healing has been gifted to me during those sound sessions.

After the workshop, I listen to the sound track daily as instructed. As tears rolled down my cheeks, I felt like I was missing home, which I did not understand at all. I was shown how the gift continues to develop. I was also shown bits and pieces of life as a Hathor. Then I was like, "Umm . . . what?" Finally, I knew it was time to ask my Records.

This time in my Records, I set the intention to connect with the star lineage information. At first, I was in the dimension with the ocean of light and Light Beings around me as before. Then I was being greeted by a Light Being who escorted me into another room and started to do some measurement on me. It felt like when you go to the doctor's office and the nurse measures your height, weight, and blood pressure. But I understood that they were measuring the level of star lineage in me or something like that.

Next they opened up a door into yet another room with a hallway in the middle and surrounded by movie screens on both sides. It was like going to a museum where both walls have moving displays and you see them while walking down the middle. That was exactly what I did; I walked through this hallway in this room with movies playing on both sides. By the way, those movies were definitely like sci-fi movies and not Earth realm at all.

At the end of the hallway, I came to another door. I walked through that door and came back to the same space with the ocean of light and Light Beings around me where I had started. As soon as I settled in the middle of the Light Beings, all the different Light Beings popped up and filled the entire space up and down and no longer just at the floor level.

Then I asked very specific questions about my star lineage with regard to Hathor and Arcturian. My Records provided me with so much more details this time than the last time, when I had simply asked a general question.

The visual images were shown to me in a way that I could understand and that was necessary in order for my human brain to translate the information. How everyone receives the information is different, as the information meets each person wherever they are.

My experience just happened yesterday, the day before Thanksgiving, which is the day I'm writing this chapter. The Records wanted me to include this piece of information in the book. At first I thought all this stuff about star lineage might come across as a bit extreme and might be too weird or shocking for readers, but I decided to follow the guidance and trust that you will find it helpful.

How did I know providing introduction of star lineage information in this book was not driven by my non-integrated ego? The easiest way to help you understand is to describe how I felt. I did not feel emotional, not excited, anxious, nor scared. I wrote this in a very neutral and detached state of mind. There is a sense of knowing that this information belongs in this book.

I am offering my Unlock the Door video series as my gift to you, to thank you for reading and to help you set a solid foundation for your Akashic journey. Go to www.akashicrecordskey.com to sign up.

CHAPTER SEVEN

ACCESS THE AKASHIC RECORDS FOR NON-HUMANS

Before you start, please review Chapter 3 on the prayer instruction and Chapter 4 on the guidelines.

Applications – Non-human

Since the Akashic Records exist everywhere, everything, human, animal, or inanimate, has its own Records as well. With proper permission, the Akashic Records can be accessed for pets, buildings, businesses, and places, to name a few most common ones.

There are many applications and it is impossible to list them all. If you're unsure of how and whether to try accessing the

Akashic Records in a way not mentioned in this book, the best thing is to seek information from your own Records and not from others. Information that is relevant to you will be revealed from your Records. Or you can ask your Records about the best way to proceed.

General Examples of Applications

Open your pet's Records to understand why it is mischievous. Permission from your pet is required. As I mentioned in the guidelines earlier, look at your pets in the eyes and ask your dogs or cats if they want a reading. If they walk away, that means no. If they stay, that means yes. After reading the prayer out loud once, set the intention to open the Records of your pet by thinking something like, "I would like to access the Records of my dog."

Open the Records of your house to see how it wants to be improved or changed. No permission is required if you own or rent the property or live there permanently. After reading the prayer out loud once, set the intention to open the Records of your house. Just think "I would like to access the Records of my house."

Remember the intention, and not the specific name, makes the consciousness move. If you have more than one dog, the easiest way to specify which dog is by name. Similarly, if you have more than one house, you need to specify which house. You can specify in any way as long as you know which house it is. The easiest way is to specify by location such as a state or a town.

Open the Records of your business to find the best way to market it. No permission is required if you own the business. After reading the prayer out loud once, set the intention to open the Records of your business.

Open the Records of a crystal to find out about its history, properties, and journey. No permission is required if you own the crystal. After reading the prayer out loud once, set the intention to open the Records of this crystal.

Open the Records of a National Park. No permission is required since it is a public place. After reading the prayer out loud once, set the intention to open the Records of XYZ Park.

You might notice that the energy of the Akashic Records of non-human animals or things is different from that of human beings.

Specific Examples of Applications

A student of mine opened the Akashic Records of a bonsai tree that he'd had for over 35 years. The bonsai had started dying, and he wanted to know why. The Records of this tree let him know that the tree had heard his conversation with his wife about selling their house, the need to downsize, and items they were not going to bring to the new house. The bonsai tree was one of them. Therefore, the bonsai tree was thinking it was time for it to go, hence, dying.

Another student of mine opened the Records of a singing bowl she had bought. She wanted to know where it had been made and the places it had been. She got that it was made in Tibet. It spent its early life in a Buddhist monastery and was used for chanting meditation rituals. Later, it ended up being moved into a private home.

During my presidency of the New Haven chapter of the Holistic Chamber of Commerce, our chapter wanted to host a holistic fair. None of our leadership team member had experience with such a big event. In addition to seeking help from experts, we consulted the Akashic Records of our chapter. We asked for guidance from the Records on many things, such as where to find the best location, the most effective way to advertise, how to boost the energy for the event, how many volunteers we needed, how much money we should charge the vendors, etc. The guidance from the Records was extremely helpful during our planning and the fair turned out to be very successful.

After the fire, I opened the Records of my house. I was shown visual images indicating that my house was scared, shaking, and confused. My house worried if it had been abandoned since I no longer lived there and everything was removed from it. Based on that information, I did many energy healing sessions on my house. When I opened up the Records again, the house was calm and stable. There was even a sense of my house acknowledging the extended period of time needed for restoration, and acknowledging that it will remain being patient until my return. It is such a great feeling knowing that the energy of my house is now calm after the turmoil.

While being displaced from my home since the fire, it has come to my attention that I missed the land dearly. Wanting to understand why, I opened the Records of my property, the land itself. I saw that in several past lifetimes, I had lived on this same land. I was also shown the positive effect of my energy healing on the land since the fire. The energy healing was able to release many karma imbalances, raise the vibration of the land, and activate the sacred geometry of the land.

When I suffered from writer's block at the very beginning of writing this book, I ask my Records and the Records of this book what was behind my struggle. I was shown lots of fear about writing something that is totally new and different from what I've learned from others before, as well as fear of being ridiculed. I had to overcome my fears. So before I wrote each chapter of this book, I opened the Records of this book and mapped out an outline for each chapter. I then confirmed with the Records of this book the necessity of each topic and its impact on you, the reader. Therefore, with the exception of the introduction of my story, the entire book is given by the Records.

Just Do It! Open Records Exercise #5 – Non-human

Pick a non-human item that you have questions about for this exercise. Your home or pet are good choices for your first non-human practice.

Just so you don't have to page through this book to find it, here is the prayer again for you to use:

The Universal Akashic Prayer© (UAP)

Dear Universal Light Beings,

We hold your love, light, and wisdom in our hearts.

Please help us to be a clear channel with complete trust

in our ability to surrender our human judgment.

Please help us to connect with open hearts,

And to know the truth of our existence.

So that we may be of service for the highest good of all.

Open Records:

1. Read the prayer once out loud. You can read it twice out loud if you feel the need.

2. Set the intention that you would like to access the Akashic Records of whichever item you pick. Do this in your head without saying it out loud.

3. Visualize the light of this item's Akashic Records coming down from your eighth chakra (approximately at arm's length when you raise your arms above your head) to your heart. It connects your heart to your will at the solar plexus area (below your heart and above your belly button). It then connects your heart to the divine (above your eighth chakra).

4. Use your imagination or in your mind's eye (in the middle of your brow) to observe your surroundings. Notice them and let them go.

5. In your mind, ask the Universal Light Beings to show you their presence in any way that you could notice. Observe and let it go.

Ask questions that you have in mind:

6. In your mind, tell your Records what you want to explore, one question at a time. You can describe the situation to get the perfect match information from the Records. Wait for five minutes for information to flow through.

Close Records:

7. If you feel complete. Express gratitude to the Universal Light Beings. Say, "We are complete" out loud to end the exercise.

8. Write down what you get from the Records.

If you are opening the Akashic Records of a non-human

item for someone else, then you will facilitate the conversation between your client and the Akashic Records of the item by asking questions out loud.

Your clients will tell you the questions they have in mind. You will then help them to clarify those questions and verbally communicate to your clients the information you receive from the Records.

For the closing part, you will ask if the client feels complete before you express gratitude and say, "We are complete" to end the exercise.

CHAPTER EIGHT

ACCESS THE AKASHIC RECORDS FOR OTHER PEOPLE

Before you start, please review Chapter 3 on the prayer instruction and Chapter 4 on the guidelines.

What You Will Need

Self-Work:

When you let people know you have been spending time cleaning and organizing your house and that it's so much better to live in now, do you ever have people jokingly ask, "When can you come to my house?"

Well, of course you won't be able to help them until you finish your own house. And you are probably not going to do the actual house cleaning for them. Instead, you'd give them ideas and suggestions for how they could organize their house.

Being an Akashic Records Advisor is a little like that. You have to work on your own issues first before you can help others to do the same. The more you work through your own issues, the higher your consciousness level, the clearer a channel you become, and the more skillful you are at asking questions. All of these enhance your working relationship with the Records and the clarity of information so that you can better help people.

This is not saying that you can't help others until you have no more issues—that's impossible, anyway. You just need to have more experience with working through your own issues than other people have with theirs.

Therefore, it is not unusual to find that all of a sudden you are seeing clients with similar problems. This is often the Universe's way of bringing to our awareness what we need to work on next.

Trust:

We already talked about the importance of getting self-centeredness, and particularly self-doubt, out of the way. If it is difficult for you to trust the information you receive, a good way to overcome that is to convey information without thinking and hesitation. As soon as you receive something, go ahead and describe it without giving your mind a chance to doubt yourself.

I found it helpful to use a digital voice recorder and practice with that in my own Akashic Records. I opened my Records and then did the whole session speaking out loud and describing the information as soon as it showed up. You could also practice with your reading partners or friends. Overtime, you will gain more clarity on the information. When you raise your confidence, you create a positive cycle that just keeps repeating.

A Servant's Heart:

The Akashic Records granted us access for the highest good of everyone and everything. The sixth line of the prayer says it all: "So that we may be of service for the highest good of all."

It is a privilege and honor to be trusted by someone to access their Records. As Akashic Records advisors, we are to serve and help people. We are not an authority figure over the client to lecture the client on what they should or shouldn't do. We are merely a clear channel to facilitate healing for the client's highest good and to convey information when the client is ready to receive. Choose your words wisely and use your voice compassionately. Again, consistent practice with the Records is the key to getting there.

Educate Clients Before the Session:

Your clients might not know what the Akashic Records are or how the Akashic Records advice session is different from other readings. To avoid frustration on both sides, make sure your clients understand the differences. It is helpful to provide the clients with a written document to help them better prepare before the session.

Examples of Accessing the Akashic Records for Others

People seek out your help for many reasons. One common thread is that they come to you because there is something that either affects their lives greatly or troubles them deeply, and they hope to move beyond that. It could be they are at a decision point or having a difficult relationship. They might be looking for help with financial issues, career challenges, health problems, grieving, trauma, business strategies, and more.

To help the people that you are meant to help, it is important to be clear on what the Akashic Records advice session is not, so that you know whether what the client needs is a right fit for the service you offer. If not, it is your responsibility to let them know.

The Akashic Records are a tool for personal development and growth. It is a healing session that helps your clients know themselves at the inner core level while hidden truth is being revealed to them and the information is conveyed.

It requires that the clients be actively engaged in the conversation and provide specifics on the situation they would like to explore.

The Akashic Records are not for prediction, curiosity, speculation, psychic work, mediumship, or replacing medical, legal, or financial advice.

"When will I meet the love of my life?", "Is he or she my soul mate?", "Should I get a divorce?", "Should I quit my job?", or "Should I buy this house?" are not the type of questions that will help a person to know himself/herself at a deeper level and learn.

Part of your skill set as an Akashic Records advisor is to navigate the conversation to find out from the client why she/he is asking the question. This usually leads to hidden agendas that the Records want the person to be aware of. Take these types of questions and ask the Records in a different way. Your skills will develop as you consistently work with the Records.

Akashic Records Advisor Open Records Exercise #6 - Self

The purpose of this exercise is to seek guidance from your Records on what things might be in the way of you becoming the best advisor you can be and how to overcome them.

Just so you don't have to page through this book to find it, here is the prayer again for you to use:

The Universal Akashic Prayer© (UAP)

Dear Universal Light Beings,

We hold your love, light, and wisdom in our hearts.

Please help us to be a clear channel with complete trust

in our ability to surrender our human judgment.

Please help us to connect with open hearts,

And to know the truth of our existence.

So that we may be of service for the highest good of all.

Open Records:

1. Read the prayer once out loud. You can read it twice out loud if you feel the need.

2. Set the intention that you would like to access your Akashic Records. Do this in your head and don't say it out loud.

3. Visualize the light of your Akashic Records coming down from your eighth chakra (approximately at arm's length when you raise your arms above your head) to your heart. It connects your heart to your will at the solar plexus area (below your heart and above your belly button). It then connects your heart to the divine (above your eighth chakra).

4. Use your inner eye (your third eye in the middle of the brow) to observe your surroundings. Notice them and let them go.

5. In your mind, ask the Universal Light Beings to show you their presence in any way that you could notice. Observe and let it go.

Ask questions:

6. In your mind, tell your Records that you want to explore what things might be preventing you from becoming the best advisor you can be.

7. Ask your Records to show you in any way you could understand.

8. If you do not understand, then tell your Records that and ask them to show you in a different way.

9. Wait for five minutes for information to flow through.

10. Next ask your Records if they have any suggestions for how you can overcome any blocks.

11. If you do not understand, then tell your Records that and ask them to show you in a different way.

12. Wait for five minutes for information to flow through.

Close Records:

13. Express gratitude to the Universal Light Beings. Say, "We are complete" out loud to end the exercise.

14. Write down what you get from the Records.

A recording of this guided exercise is included in Unlock the Door series as my gift to you. You can sign up for it at www.akashicrecordskey.com.

How Does Healing Happen for Others?

I was not sure how healing happens in this realm of Akasha for other people, so I asked the Records to show me. I received, through visual images and a sense of knowing, the following description of the advisor's role and their interactions with the Records, as well as how healing happens for the client.

When the advisor reads the prayer, they open up the gateway to Akasha and bring the higher consciousness realm to the client. The Records showed me this higher dimension space surrounds both the advisor and the client.

When the advisor sets the intention to open the client's Records, the intention moves the energy of higher consciousness much like turning on a switch. The client is showered with this higher consciousness energy.

Through the conversation, the advisor assists in moving the client to the right place to receive the consciousness and information needed for healing. The Records showed me the client on a ladder; the advisor navigates and moves the ladder to the right spot in the library.

This shower of higher consciousness and information acts like a cleansing soap. When advisor's intention moves the energy of the consciousness, the effect is like using a scrubbing sponge with the cleansing soap to release the imprint and impact of life experiences that impede the client from moving forward and hence facilitate the client's healing.

The client can choose to stay in the shower or leave. Staying means the client receives truth and healing with an open heart. Leaving means the client is not ready to accept the information (the truth), which does happen from time to time.

If client chooses to leave the shower without completing an entire release for maximum healing effect, the residual imprint of limitation may require follow-up work to complete healing.

Clarification on Conscious Permission

In the reading guidelines, we talk about conscious permission being required. Conscious permission means the person has to give you permission while conscious and without any outside influence.

Therefore, we never access the Records of someone who is in coma regardless of who else gives the permission, not even the person who can legally make medical decision for them. In that situation, it is best to access the Records of the person who is asking you to intercede on behalf of the person in coma.

For example, let's say Tom comes to you and asks you to do a reading for his daughter, Mary who is in coma, because Tom wants to know what he should do about Mary's affairs. You will do a reading for Tom, instead, and ask guidance from Tom's Records on the best way for Tom to help Mary.

Here is an example about the age 18 requirement. Judy comes to you and asks you to do a reading for her son, Joe, who is 17 years, 11 months, and 29 days old. Joe has been getting into a lot of trouble in school and Judy wants to know what is going on. You will open Judy's Records instead and ask for guidance from her Records on how she can help her son. Not only her son is under age 18, but he did not give conscious permission either.

Same thing if someone asked you to do a reading for a loved one who has already passed. You will open the Records of the requester who is still alive. It is the person who is still alive in need of help instead of those who have passed.

Akashic Records Advisor Open Records Exercise #7 – Read Others

The purpose of this exercise is to give you an idea of the structure to follow when you read other people. Be very aware that this is only a simplified template. How the actual sessions with your clients will unfold is going to be different every single time. It depends mainly on the topic and skill set you acquire as an advisor through self-work and practice.

Remember the intention, and not the specific name, makes the consciousness move. Therefore, a first name to help you focus your intention on a particular person in your mind is sufficient when you are doing this for others.

Just so you don't have to page through this book to find it, here is the prayer again for you to use:

The Universal Akashic Prayer© (UAP)

Dear Universal Light Beings,

We hold your love, light, and wisdom in our hearts.

Please help us to be a clear channel with complete trust

in our ability to surrender our human judgment.

Please help us to connect with open hearts,

And to know the truth of our existence.

So that we may be of service for the highest good of all.

Open Records:

1. Read the prayer once out loud. You can read it twice out loud if you feel the need.

2. Set the intention that you would like to access the Akashic Records of your client. Using your client's first name is sufficient here. Do this in your head or say it out loud. You can observe through practice which way works best for you.

3. As the advisor, visualize the light of your client's

Akashic Records coming down from the space above both you and your client and surround you both.

4. Ask your client to visualize the light of her/his Akashic Records coming down from her/his eighth chakra (approximately at arm's length when you raise your arms above your head) to hers/his heart. It connects her/his heart to the will at the solar plexus area (below the heart and above the belly button). It then connects the heart to the divine (above the eighth chakra). This visualization helps your client shift to higher consciousness level and enhances the upcoming healing process.

As the advisor, you do this part silently for yourself:

5. Use your imagination or in your mind's eye (in the middle of your brow) to observe your surroundings.

6. In your mind, ask the Universal Light Beings to show you their presence in any way that you could notice.

7. Ask the Light Beings to help you to help your client for her/his highest good.

Note that these steps may look long but it really goes very quickly and takes just a few seconds. Of course when you first begin, you need time to practice and to feel comfortable with it.

Now, facilitate a conversation between your client and their Akashic Records through you:

8. Ask your client what they want you to help with, what

issue they want to explore in their Records. You need to make sure you only work on one question at a time. Guide the client to tell you what's going on. As they talk, pay attention to them and their Records to check on information you receive.

9. You might be prompted by their Records to ask them questions, and you might feel like you are doing detective work or probing. Please know that you are helping them to clarify their questions and getting the energy in the Akashic Records going and information flowing.

10. Verbally communicate to your client the information you receive from the Records. Remember, this is a conversation, so there will be a lot of back and forth as a two-way communication. As the conversation goes on, you will be able to get deeper to the core of the situation and truth behind it from their Records.

Close Records:

11. Ask the client if she/he feels complete. Express gratitude to the Universal Light Beings. Say, "We are complete" out loud to end the exercise.

Example of How a Session Flows – Other People

Pam came to me for an Akashic Records Consultation because she was having trouble with her boyfriend. She was thinking about leaving him, but not sure if that was the right decision. Here is a snapshot of how it went as the conversation between Pam and her Akashic Records unfolded through me:

"Tell me what is going on? How can I help you today?" I said to Pam.

"I am getting more and more unhappy with my boyfriend recently. Things are not working out and I want to know if it is time to leave him," Pam replied.

The Records asked, "What do you mean you are not happy? Can you give some example about what is bothering you?"

Pam thought a minute. "Well, silly little things that are getting on my nerves. Like not putting the toilet seat down after he uses it, or leaving the sink full of his hair after shaving, or his stuff piling up."

At this point, I was shown a visual image of a pile of clothes grown from a small pile into a big mountain and surrounded by boxes all around. So I asked Pam, "Is the pile of stuff like clothing or something else? I am seeing boxes as well. Does this mean anything to you?"

Pam sighed and said "Yes, it does. He has way too much of everything. Too many clothes, too many collections. It drives me crazy. Just the other day, a couple packages of his collection arrived and I was really mad."

I was then prompted to ask Pam, "Did you discuss this with him before? Did he know you are not happy with that?"

"Yes, I did," she said. "We've talked about it many times through our relationship. He's tried to cut down his buying volume already. Honestly, I don't know why I became so short-tempered now every time I see that packages have arrived."

Pam's Records then showed me an image of Pam in what appeared to be clothing from another era, an older time. She was holding a baby in her arms while kneeling down and begging her husband (I was made to understand that the "husband" in this image is her boyfriend now) not to leave. He went ahead and took the last bit of money they had and left the house to gamble.

The next visual shown to me was Pam burying their baby with her own two hands. I was made to understand that the baby had been sick, but she could not bring the baby to the doctor because her husband took all the money, so the baby died. I could feel that Pam was heartbroken over losing the baby and filled with rage toward her husband in that lifetime.

I communicated this image to Pam and told her what had happened in that particular past life between her and her boyfriend. I said that now, in this lifetime, her boyfriend's spending habits were triggering wounds inflicted on her from this past life. As she listened, tears ran down her face like streams of pearls. I waited; this was a critical moment in the healing process.

When Pam finally stopped crying, she looked at me and said, "I am so relieved that I now know why I have been so angry with him for not-so-obvious reasons." Pam chose to accept the truth and allow healing to continue.

Pam's hurt ran so deep that it took a couple more sessions for her to release all of that hidden anger. Since then, she has been able to gain clarity, reevaluate her relationship without the influence of the past, and make the right decision for herself.

Note that Pam was asking for a yes/no answer on whether to leave her boyfriend. It was my job to navigate the conversation to find out from Pam why she asked the question. Only then could the hidden truth behind the surface problem be revealed. Her Records wanted her to know so that she could heal from it, and she did!

CHAPTER NINE

BE THE BEST AKASHIC RECORDS ADVISOR YOU CAN BE

In the practice group for my students, I always map out reading partners for them in advance in the Records. Then, in class, I start with guided meditation in the Records. One time, I was guided to have students ask their Records for advice on what they could do to help them with their practice that day. As it happened, one student, Donna, had a partner who could not come at the last minute, so she was going to sit out. This rarely happened, since for some strange reason we have always had even numbers in the practice group. I was guided to take the place of her partner.

Donna cringed noticeably when I told her we would work together that day. Then she took a deep breath and said, "Yes, okay." I chose not to ask her what was wrong even though it was a bit strange to me. We found a quiet corner away from other students and exchanged readings.

Donna wanted to be read first. She asked about her kids. Then, when it was my turn, I asked about my family. What she got from my Records was very helpful and I gave her that feedback. That's when Donna told me that during the guided meditation at the beginning of class, she had told her Records that she was not confident or comfortable with reading others. The advice from her Records was, "Just say YES."

She was puzzled about the meaning of that until the moment she heard me saying we were going to be partners that night. The thought of reading a teacher was unsettling to Donna, but she followed the guidance she had just received from her Records, said YES, and did it. All this was a very clear message for Donna that she just needed to trust that she was in the Records.

I remember the first time I had a difficult session. Let's call the client May. May had had a very difficult life filled with trauma and abuse. She wanted to know why the same pattern happened to her over and over again. When I conveyed to her the specific reasons I got from her Records, her face froze. She stared at me and said in a very cold voice, "That is stupid. I have gone through this enough already. Why would my soul teach me by making me suffer more?

It makes no sense. I do not believe this. What is the real reason? Why? There has got to be something else."

I was still new to this work then. I could feel my heart pounding, my body tightened up, and my mind spacing out with no words to continue. I even thought of ending the session, giving her money back, and apologizing to her.

But then I remembered to ask for the support from the Light Beings to help me to know the best way to help her. Then came this from the Records: "You are in pain and angry because this hurts so much and so deeply. You just want it to go away. You have done nothing wrong. What happened to you was not a punishment. Your soul sees how perfect you are. She loves you so much and wishes you can see it too." May and I then looked at each other eye to eye for a while in silence. The session then ended after that. I had no idea whether May accepted the truth as she was leaving. That was my first lesson of learning to detach from clients' outcomes.

Clarity

No one can help everyone. Only those who you are meant to help and are able to help will come to you. Yes, including the people you think are difficult.

Have you ever seen a movie or a TV show where a character is in a situation that everyone else can see clearly except the person? Have you seen it in real life?

Truth can be unpleasant, scary, or even painful. It is normal that not everyone is ready to know the truth. You might ask, "Why does the person come to me for help in the first place if he or she is not ready to deal with truth?" When the situation is really painful, people seek help to make the pain go away, but they do not necessarily welcome the idea of dealing with more pain first in order to get to the root of the issue.

As a result, you will have difficult clients. Not once, twice, or three times. The longer you serve, the more difficult clients you will encounter. How do you prepare yourself to handle those situations?

Even though the person does not want to know the truth, their souls know it is critical for them to understand the truth in order to change the direction of their lives. You are the best person and are in the right place and at the right time to give them the truth that they need to know.

The Universe did not just send you by random luck of the draw. Get this: your soul has agreed to deliver this important message to help them *before you even incarnated into this lifetime.* Yes, it is all part of the comprehensive plan your soul and the divine made together.

You are the gardener whose job it is to plant seeds in their hearts so that when they are ready, the awareness will eventually surface. At the same time, understand that they are your teachers to expand your capacity of compassion as a person and advisor.

Therefore, when you are facing a difficult client, do your best to get yourself out of the way. With a servant's heart, ask the Light Beings to help you to help them. Ask the Light Beings what to say for their highest good in the moment.

When you work in your own Records, you know the information is not from the Records if it contains anger or judgment. Similarly, when you are working with a client and you find yourself arguing with them, insisting they do as you say, or blaming them for what's happening, these messages are definitely coming from your non-integrated ego and not the Records. You need to be able to catch yourself doing this so you can work on yourself. Spend time in your Records and ask the Light Beings to help you with it. Ask them how you can move yourself out of the way. Ask them what you can do to help yourself with this.

You are always doing your best in any given moment. You are always making progress, even though sometimes you may feel like you did a horrible job in the session. Overtime, you will notice the improvement in your skills as an advisor.

Nurturing Your Relationship with Your Own Akashic Records

Spending time and effort on building a strong relationship with your own Akashic records is the most important thing you can do in order to be a responsible advisor.

There are tons of reasons people can find to support the fact that they do not work with their Records on a regular basis.

Life happens, of course. Not enough interest, okay. Not enough time, I get it.

But out of all these reasons, there is only one truth. The truth is this work is not important to them, which is totally fine.

Really, it is fine if you are reading this book only because you are curious or just want to gain some knowledge. It is fine if you have no desire of using the Akashic Records to help navigate your own life and/or to be of service to help others. I am glad you have come across this book and hope you have enjoyed it.

However, if you would like to gain the skill set of working with the Records for either your own life or for helping others, take a deep breath. Ready? There is no way but to consistently work at it, regardless of how talented you are.

Remember the analogy that people usually don't get married on the first date! A strong relationship requires time spent together. Consciously make an effort and work with your Records, just as you would with any spiritual practice, for at least five days a week for 15 minutes. It will result in amazing progress in all aspects of your work with the Records.

Only you can experience the unequivocal difference from your own practice of before and after working consistently with your Records. You and your clients will thank you from the bottom of your and their hearts!

The more you work on yourself and the more you love and accept yourself, then the more your capacity expands to love and accept others with compassion and love. The more you raise your consciousness level with the work in your own Records, the easier it is to detach from the outcomes and release self-centeredness. Higher consciousness propels our ego to be integrated with the divine source. An integrated ego enables letting go of judgment, not only of ourselves but of others as well.

Practice, Practice, Practice makes perfect.

JUST DO IT! You will get there!

Transformation Takes Time

However you run your business is your business. Hopefully, you recognize by now that transformation takes time. The work with the Akashic Records results in a permanent, life-changing transformation. Therefore, long-term support to your clients is extremely important. You will want your clients to have the option of working with you long-term, versus a single session, so that you can support them throughout their journey.

For a very skillful and experienced advisor, the relationship with a long-term client's Records can be strong enough that you can access information without the client's active, verbal, real-time engagement and get the answer to a very simple question. Clients who are going through a lot of shifting and changes might need this kind of support from you to check something for them quickly from their Records, versus a full session, so that they can move forward quickly for the highest good of all. You are the only person who can decide whether you are skilled and comfortable enough to do this for your clients. When in doubt, ask your Records.

Equally important is to recognize that this is also a form of service, even though it is "just" a quick check for information. If this situation does happen in your practice, it is best to set up the scope of your services and associated pricing first to make sure there is an even exchange of energy in which both parties have clarity and boundaries are properly maintained.

All and all, you will need to be clear on the value you provide and what feels right in your heart. And, yes, check with your Records.

Boundaries and Self-Care

The client's journey is their own. Whether or not clients are going to make a change in their life is not up to you, but them. It is not your responsibility.

Your job is to raise your consciousness level as high as possible so you can be a clear channel for the Light, facilitate healing, and convey the information for the highest good of your client.

We are human. We all experience life's ups and downs. Just because you are on a spiritual journey working with the Akashic Records does not mean that you have your own life all figured out. You have your fair share of challenges in your life just as everyone else.

There will be times when you will feel the need to be with yourself, to rest, reflect, or release. Please honor your own emotions and space, allow yourself time to process, and say no to appointments or giving the help people seek from you.

Only by taking care of yourself, from the inside out, can you be the best advisor for others.

To thank you for reading and to help you become the best advisor you can be, I'm offering my Unlock the Door video series free as my gift to you. Go to www.akashicrecordskey.com to sign up for it.

CHAPTER TEN

CONCLUSION

For nine weeks, I worked on this book. It is surreal that I am writing the final chapter now on the first day of December 2016. It is even wilder looking back to where I was in August, when the signs from the Universe and nudges from my Records coincided to make me pause and pay attention.

They want this book written.

I have shared with you plenty of my fears and challenges that could have stopped me from writing this book. It is the belief and trust that I hold dearly that gave me the courage to overcome them. First and by far the most, I trust my Records, as they have not steered me wrong once.

We are all here for a reason. I do not need to know why I am here but I sure am not going to chicken out on any chance to realize the highest potential that my soul can achieve in this lifetime. If there is anything I can do to contribute to the hope and future of this world we all live in, I can't let my fears stop me.

How about you, my dear fellow travelers?

Would you like to be a force in the healing of the Earth that supports your life?

Would you like to realize the highest potential of your soul?

Would you like to know the truth of your existence?

From this book, you have learned what the Akashic Records are, how can they help you, the Universal Akashic Prayer©, guidelines to access, how to access the Akashic Records for yourself and for others, how to move yourself out of the way, and how to be the best Akashic Records advisor you can be.

If you find yourself not interested in the book after the first time reading it, then this book is not the right fit for you. I thank you for picking it up in the first place.

If you find this book resonates with you, then the content of this book is meant to be reread many times throughout the journey to help you process your experience. It will be helpful to reread the book from time to time as you gain more experience in the Records. As your consciousness level rises, so will your understanding of the content. You will discover new information each time you read it.

I highly recommend that you keep a journal and write down your experiences in the Records. You will be in awe at how far you have come when you look back.

If you intend to use this book to help others in addition to yourself, please honor this Sacred Contract of helping others by doing everything in your power to be the best advisor you can be.

No matter where you are on your journey. Please know that you are not alone. We are all in this together. We are all helping each other and doing our best.

My wish for you is that you have found or will find someone to share this Akashic journey with, to cheer you on with your adventure in this lifetime, to support you and hold space for you.

If you are looking for more support in addition to this book, you can look into my Akashic Records Explorer Certification Program developed based on this book at www.akashicrecordskey.com. At the end of the program, you will be able to access the Akashic Records for yourself and for others. This enables you to receive insights from the soul and make better decisions in life for the right next step. You will know how to best communicate with your Records and build a strong connection with your soul so that the information will come easier, quicker, and clearer.

I truly hope you have enjoyed the book and find it helpful to your journey.

Love and Blessings,

Jiayuh Chyan

RESOURCES

Testing the Vibrational Level of the Prayer

Since the Universal Akashic Prayer© was given for writing this book, it was important to have other people try it out. Here is some of the feedback on the prayer from people who work with the Akashic Records on a regular basis.

From Rose-Ann C. Chrzanowski, Akashic Records Advisor, Reiki Master Teacher, Ordained Minister, and Justice of the Peace:

> *My dear Jiayuh,*
>
> *I love the new prayer and am honored that you sent it to me. I had to try it out immediately. I love it!*
>
> *Everything I learned about the Akashic Records and accessing them is fascinating and enlightening. Like all learning opportunities, the process is evolving and growing. The new prayer fills me with hope and peace.*

It's beautiful in its simplicity and makes me feel like I am truly working in partnership with the Universal Light Beings to find answers to my questions and clarity of my life's journey. I am grateful for the higher vibration. I feel elevated using this prayer. It deepens levels of meditation and opens the channels of communication. This prayer gives me a wonderful feeling of open conversation that heightens understanding. When I used it for the first time, I felt I connect and hear faster and clearer. I felt welcomed and celebrated, comfortable and peaceful.

From Sheila Holland, Akashic Records Advisor, and Energy Medicine Practitioner:

Hi Lynne!

Here are my thoughts on the new prayer. Tell Jiayuh I wish her all the best with her book!

This prayer is both inspirational and empowering. It has been channeled from a higher level of consciousness than others I have experienced. The simplicity of the prayer invites each one of us, whatever our level of consciousness, to participate. I feel how powerfully the words reflect the connection between the participant and all people as well as to the Light Beings that they are calling on for guidance. This simple and powerful channeling does not imply that anyone needs to rely on the power of someone else's prayer or channeling in order to access what they need from the spiritual realm; therein lies the source of its loving power. It invites all who use it to experience a deeper sense of their own empowerment and connection to all that is.

From Ofelia Dulko, Akashic Records Advisor and Energy Medicine Practitioner:

First try in the Records on Wednesday, November 2, 2016.

Prayer is very simple. I found I had no conflicts with the words, phrasing or concepts. I was aware of my heart center more than usual. The place where I ended up was different then the few I usually experience when I open my records. This was just me in a plain white space. I saw nothing else.

I felt peace, and was aware of pure potentiality in this space. I asked my questions and I received clear, helpful information. It was only for five minutes and then I closed my records.

My only addition at this time is that I would and did include deep gratitude in my closing. The "we are complete" just didn't cut it for me.

Day 6 in the Records, Monday, November 7, 2016.

Went into records with your prayer after own version

of opening the heart. Asked the question "how can I be of service to the world?" Was shown an image of my interior self as a wood stove that had embers in it but the fire needed stoking. I understood that I have to build up my energy/vibration within so that I can be a beacon for others. Was reminded of a breathing method I have practiced in the past. I began to practice that and the fire began to burn bright.

Stayed in the records for a bit and meditated and closed.

I then decided to go into my records with the old prayer. Upon finishing the prayer I saw the old familiar steps and walked in and asked the same question at the desk. I was shown to a different room and sat in the only chair in the middle of the room, I saw myself with this same light inside, but was also shown myself bowing to myself in the chair. When I questioned what was going on, I was told yet again; it does not matter what prayer or method we use to connect with spirit. What matters is how pure our intentions are and that we honor the source and have gratitude.

This is my last entry as this exercise feels complete to me. I hope this information is helpful. Please feel free to call me if you need further explanation of my experiences.

Much luck and much love to you.

ACKNOWLEDGMENTS

Ten years ago, if anyone told me that I would be doing the type of work I am doing now, let alone writing a book on the Akashic Records, I would have run the opposite way.

Every single person that has come into my life, be it for a season or a lifetime, has helped me to get to where I am. There is not enough physical space to mention every name here. There is, however, an overwhelming amount of gratitude in my heart for every one of you. I thank you for coming in and making an impact on my life.

I am grateful for my father. He was such a bright light and shone it everywhere he went with his big heart, helping people. He was a basketball coach and then a high school principle for over 35 years until his passing. All his life, he educated and helped both teachers and students to have a better life. He paid particularly close attention to students having trouble at home and talked to them whenever he could. Growing up, we even had a student living with us through high school because her parents would not raise her or pay for school.

My dad is also one of my spiritual guides. In the beginning of my spiritual journey there was so much heartache that I had to heal from. His love is the reason that I made it through. Thank you, Dad. I love you too!

Thank you, Mum, for taking care of me when I was often sick as a child. Every penny you saved allowed me to complete graduate school in the US. I would not have had that life experience without your sacrifice. I wish I could make more trips to Taiwan and see you. I love you, Mum.

Gratitude to my ex-husband, as our marriage was the catalyst of my awakening.

Two of my close friends, Deborah Fountas and Karen Leddy, were there for me while I went through divorce. They taught me American etiquette so I would know how to fit in. Thank you for treating me like family.

Thank you, Kathleen Greco, for following guidance and inviting me to your home for breakfast when I was a stranger. I cherish our friendship.

Heartfelt thanks to my former psychotherapist, Sharon Diaz. Thank you for introducing me to Energy Medicine and helping me to uncover hidden scars. Thank you for being the lifeline on the phone while I was overseas dealing with a family crisis and beside myself.

Thank you, Jeanne Zuzel, for being a great teacher of Healing Touch and answering all of my questions patiently.

Thank you, Pat Zainc, for believing in me all along when I had no clue myself and supporting me through tough times.

Thank you, Gene Ang, for being a great mentor and opening the Arcturian Healing world and more to me.

Thank you, Linda Howe, for bringing out the Akashic Records leadership quality in me. Without your work, I would not be where I am with the Records.

Words can't express my gratitude for Patty Collinsworth, my mentor and very first Akashic Records teacher. Your trust, support, and love throughout the milestones and growing pains on my Akashic Journey are the reasons that I believe in myself to fulfill my divine mission. I am forever grateful.

Thank you, Diane Lavin, for watching out for me and giving me your honest opinions for my highest good.

If it were not for my experience in developing curriculum with my colleagues at The Akashic Network, it would be totally inconceivable to me that I would have the ability to write this book. My heartfelt thanks to Fran Friedman, Lynne Grobsky, Gwendolyn Hill, and Laura Hosford, and for the work we have done together. Special thanks to Lynne for always being there for me as I navigate through curves and bumps while shifting to the next best version of myself.

Thank you, Chet, for accepting and loving me as I was. I am grateful for your encouragement, which helped me to spread my wings and reach higher.

I cannot thank my editor, Maggie McReynolds, enough. You have the most remarkably keen eyes to see the missing links, and the magic to edit my book into a beautiful, flowing river of truth that shines even more brightly. Thank you!

Last but not the least; I want to thank my publisher, Angela Lauria. There were many tender moments and doubting times when I did not think I was going to make it. Angela showed me the way and held the space for me so that I could walk through the door myself and come out as the author of this book. I am forever grateful for your dedication. Thank you for believing in me.

ABOUT THE
AUTHOR

Jiayuh Chyan is an Akashic Records Teacher, Multidimensional Healing Facilitator, Energy Medicine Practitioner, and the founder of Jiayuh Chyan. Through the Akashic Records, Sacred Geometry, and Universal stars healing frequency, Jiayuh offers programs that provide her students and clients with the knowledge and tools that result in permanent, life-changing transformation.

Jiayuh holds a Master's Degree in Applied Mathematics – Actuarial Science from The University of Illinois at Urbana-Champaign. She worked as an actuary in her former career.

For over a decade, Jiayuh has been helping people live a happier and more effective life. She has a Multidimensional Healing radio show on News for the Soul network.

With her guidance, her students are able to build a strong relationship with the Akashic Records, access it with confidence, and, with a higher consciousness level, receive information that helps them navigate their own life as well as their clients'. Her clients are able to discover the hidden truth behind issues in their lives, gain clarity and new perspectives, and make changes that bring them meaning and joy.

Jiayuh's work with her own Records has supported her unlikely success every step of the way through crisis and milestones. Her Records were instrumental in helping her to make the right decision to leave corporate America and pursue her passion of helping people, develop her Akashic Records curriculum, realize the importance of reclaiming her birth name Jiayuh, function through the aftermath of her house fire, and fulfill her divine mission of writing this book to spread the Light.

Jiayuh loves cooking and enjoys singing nostalgic folk songs in Chinese. She lives in Prospect, Connecticut. Connect with her at www.akashicrecordskey.com.

THANK YOU

It is my hope that this book will reach the hands of people who have been seeking information that is brought through by the Universal Akashic Prayer©. I am honored that you took the time to read this book.

There is no coincidence in life. You might not know the reason why you are reading this right now, but it is up to you to find out if you choose to.

To help you further along on your Akashic journey, I created my Unlock the Door companion audio/video series to go with this book. Items in the Unlock the Door series are hand-picked from my Akashic Records Explorer Certification Program that can help you move forward. Go to www.akashicrecordskey.com to sign up for it.

UNLOCK THE DOOR:

- **FREE GUIDED LIGHT MEDITATION:** This audio recording of a guided Light Meditation helps you prepare energetically for the work in the Records.

- **FREE GUIDED OPEN RECORDS EXERCISE:** This is an audio recording of a guided Open Records exercise #6. The purpose of this exercise is to seek guidance from your Records on what is in the way of you becoming the best Akashic Records advisor you can be and how to overcome these obstacles.

- **FREE VIDEO CLASS:** This two-part class will help you to get clarity on your next step of your Akashic journey.

- **FREE STRATEGY SESSION:** Would you like to have ongoing support in addition to this book? If you are interested in my Akashic Records Explorer Certification Program developed based on this book, let's talk and find out if we are meant to work together. You can get started by filling out the form here: www.akashicrecordskey.com/free-strategy-session/.

difference press

Difference Press offers entrepreneurs, including life coaches, healers, consultants, and community leaders, a comprehensive solution to get their books written, published, and promoted. A boutique-style alternative to self-publishing, Difference Press boasts a fair and easy-to-understand profit structure, low-priced author copies, and author-friendly contract terms. Its founder, Dr. Angela Lauria, has been bringing to life the literary ventures of hundreds of authors-in-transformation since 1994.

LET'S MAKE A DIFFERENCE WITH YOUR BOOK

You've seen other people make a difference with a book. Now it's your turn. If you are ready to stop watching and start taking massive action, reach out.

"Yes, I'm ready!"

In a market where hundreds of thousands books are published every year and are never heard from again, all participants of The Author Incubator have bestsellers that are actively changing lives and making a difference.

"In two years we've created over 250 bestselling books in a row, 90% from first-time authors." We do this by selecting the highest quality and highest potential applicants for our future programs.

Our program doesn't just teach you how to write a book—our team of coaches, developmental editors, copy editors, art directors, and marketing experts incubate you from book idea to published bestseller, ensuring that the book you create can actually make a difference in the world. Then we give you the training you need to use your book to make the difference you want to make in the world, or to create a business out of serving your readers. If you have life-or world-changing ideas or services, a servant's heart, and the willingness to do what it REALLY takes to make a difference in the world with your book, go to http://theauthorincubator.com/apply/ to complete an application for the program today.

OTHER BOOKS BY DIFFERENCE PRESS

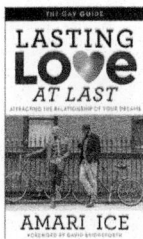

Lasting Love At Last: The Gay Guide To Attracting the Relationship of Your Dreams

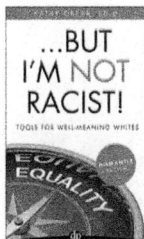

by Amari Ice

...But I'm Not Racist!: Tools for Well-Meaning Whites

by Kathy Obear

Who the Fuck Am I To Be a Coach: A Warrior's Guide to Building a Wildly Successful Coaching Business From the Inside Out

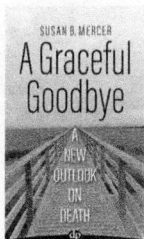

by Megan Jo Wilson

A Graceful Goodvye: A New Outlook on Death

by Susan B. Mercer

Standing Up: From Renegade Professor to Middle-Aged Comic

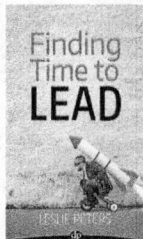

by Ada Cheng

Finding Time to Lead: Seven Practices to Unleash Outrageous Potential

by Leslie Peters

CPSIA information can be obtained
at www.ICGtesting.com
Printed in the USA
LVOW03s0032030118
561598LV00002B/4/P